THE ULTIMATE

KIDS' ADVENTURE GUIDE TO CHICAGO

Library of Congress Control Number: 2016962279
ISBN: 9781681060774

Design by Jill Halpin

Printed in the United States of America
17 18 19 20 21   5 4 3 2 1

Please note that websites, phone numbers, addresses, and company names are subject to change or cancellation. We did our best to relay the most accurate information available, but due to circumstances beyond our control, please do not hold us liable for misinformation. When exploring new destinations, please do your homework before you go.

THE ULTIMATE

KIDS' ADVENTURE GUIDE TO CHICAGO

SARAH PARISI

I dedicate this book to my parents; to John,
my husband and partner-in-everything;
and to my kids—Cooper, Dexter,
and Campbell—who inspired both our
adventures and this book.
Thank you all for your constant support.

✳ TABLE OF CONTENTS ✳

✳ INTRODUCTION ✳

Having children changes your perspective and makes everything new again, and having kids helped reinvigorate my love of exploring the truly amazing city of Chicago. It's important to me that my children learn their way around the city and learn to really appreciate the resources and attractions that are right here in their own backyard—things that many people travel great distances to experience. So, we began adventuring.

We loved discovering new places and comparing them with places we'd been before. We shared recommendations with other parents and didn't shy away from long drives. Eventually I decided I wanted to share our experiences with even more people, so I created a resource blog for families called Toddling Around Chicagoland. Over the years, we've had some wonderful adventures that eventually led to the opportunity to write this guidebook. I'm so excited to share some of the phenomenal places we've discovered, and I encourage other families to do the same.

This guidebook is intended to help families traveling to Chicago with children to prepare for and enjoy their trip, and to serve as a resource for families who live in or near Chicago. Of course, fun doesn't stop at the city limits, so this book doesn't either; there are amazing "Chicago" attractions that aren't even in the city boundaries.

My hope is that this book will encourage families to try new things and explore all areas of the city and suburbs. I've included information about a wide variety of activities—from traditionally family-friendly businesses like play cafés and children's museums, to not-so-traditional choices, like roller derby games and indoor skydiving—for a variety of ages, budgets, and interests. I've learned so much along the way to further our exploration!

Also, a few notes:

- I did my very best to include accurate, current information, but things change. Do a little research before you go if you have your heart set on a particular activity, or be prepared to amend your plans and be open to new adventures.

- Parking in the city, especially in the downtown and Loop areas, can be difficult and/or expensive. Online websites or apps like Park Whiz or SpotHero allow you to find and reserve discounted parking before you arrive at your destination.

- Public libraries and park districts are fantastic resources—for events, activities, and possibly even free or discounted tickets to attractions. Check them out before you travel!

- Discounts are available at many museums and cultural attractions. If you're a resident of the city of Chicago or a resident of the state of Illinois, a member of the military or a veteran, a student, a teacher, or an EBT (Electronic Benefits Transfer) card holder, inquire about whether any special discounts apply.

- Membership in museums or institutions can sometimes entitle you to free or discounted admission at other attractions, even if they're attractions in another city or state. If you are a member of any museums or institutions, inquire about reciprocal programs.

- A map of all the things to do included in this book can be found at http://bit.ly/KidsGuideChgoMapDo

- A map of all the places to stay included in this book can be found at http://bit.ly/KidsGuideChgoMapStay

- A map of seasonal fairs and festivals included in this book can be found at http://bit.ly/KidsGuideChgoMapFairs

• A map of day trip locations included in this book can be found at http://bit.ly/KidsGuideChgoMapDayTrips

This is just a starting point for me and for you. There are more attractions, restaurants, and events in the Windy City than could ever be included in one book, so I encourage you to explore beyond my suggestions here! I'd love to hear your thoughts on this book, your experiences visiting places I've included, and any of your new discoveries. You can find me blogging on ToddlingAroundChicagoland.com, on Twitter and Instagram at @ToddlingChicago, or by email at toddlingchicago@yahoo.com.

PLACES TO STAY

★ CHICAGO ★

Downtown Chicago is the obvious choice for places to stay. Hotels are plentiful, and many boast amazing views, grand accommodations, and an abundance of attractions within walking distance. There are so many benefits to staying in the heart of the city. You can stay in a world-class historic building right in the middle of everything and bask in the energy and atmosphere of Chicago. Premier dining can be found in Chicago hotels or, just steps away, you can enjoy countless attractions within walking distance, and travel almost anywhere in the city using easily accessible public transportation. Many downtown hotels cater to families and will provide packages in conjunction with local attractions, or provide amenities you couldn't dream up on your own, making the hotel stay a highlight of the trip rather than just a place to sleep between activities.

EMBASSY SUITES
600 N. State Street, Chicago, IL 60654
(312) 943-3800
www.embassysuiteschicago.com

Traveling with kids can be stressful, especially when your entire family is confined to one room. Embassy Suites has two-room suites allowing a little more space and privacy for everyone. (Single rooms are also available.) Free hot breakfast and an evening reception with drinks and snacks adds convenience and savings. There are two Italian restaurants on-site, and they have a 24-hour gym and indoor pool. Located at Ohio and State Streets, Embassy Suites is the perfect hub for all your Chicago adventures—The Art Institute, Water Tower Place, Navy Pier, the Shedd Aquarium, the Hancock, Willis Tower, and Lincoln Park Zoo are all within three miles. Looking for something special? There are packages geared toward families, like a Field Museum package and an American Girl package, and spa services are available.

Rates start at about $100.
The CTA Red Line train stops at Grand and State, about a block away.
Valet parking is about $60 a night; parking in the Millennium Garage is about $45.

FOUR SEASONS
120 E. Delaware Place, Chicago, IL 60611
(312) 280-8800
www.fourseasons.com/chicago

Sometimes a hotel is just a place to lay your head at the end of a busy day, but sometimes it's one of the highlights of the trip. The Four Seasons is a five-star luxury hotel with awe-inspiring views of the skyline and the lake. The Four Seasons has its very own art collection, including works by Andy Warhol and Henri Matisse. They also have a spa, fitness center, and an indoor pool. (Fun fact: The pool at the Four Seasons in Chicago was where they filmed the scene in *Home Alone 2* where Kevin lost his shorts!)

The Four Seasons really caters to families, offering a variety of services including a teen spa, a pizza-making class for teens, a kids' clubroom, babysitting, and a Family Fun Package with special perks. Need an extra bed? For a $40 fee they can put an extra bed in a king room. Best of all, you can request a complimentary visit from the "Ice Cream Man," who will come to your room to serve sundaes to the kids!

If you can drag yourself out of the Four Seasons, you can do it in style—the hotel offers a complimentary luxury car service that, when available, will take you to your destination within two miles of the hotel.

Rates start at about $445.

The Four Seasons is about half a mile away from the Chicago stop of the CTA Red Line train. Multiple CTA bus routes stop along Michigan at Chestnut, a couple blocks away.

Valet parking is available for about $70 a night.

HOTEL PALOMAR
505 N. State Street, Chicago, IL 60654
(312) 755-9703
www.hotelpalomar-chicago.com

This four-star River North boutique hotel is blocks away from Michigan Avenue shopping. Pets are welcome, and they have an extensive list of amenities, including laundry and dry cleaning, a fitness center, in-room dining, and spa services. Each room has a yoga mat, and yoga classes are available.

Hotel Palomar is part of the Kimpton family of hotels, which offers the Kimpton Kids program. Kids checking in can receive a welcome gift and animal-print bathrobes for use during their stay. Accredited babysitters are available, and you can also request outlet covers and other child safety products, cribs, play-yards, and child safety seats. Need more than that? Ask about equipment rental of strollers, scooters, and other family gear. They also have a "Guppy Love" Program in which kids can have a fish in their room during their stay. Room options include rooms with queen- or king-size beds, one-bedroom suites, luxury suites, or an artist suite.

Rates start at about $169.

Take the Red Line train to Grand and State Streets.

Valet parking is about $60.

JAMES HOTEL

55 E. Ontario Street, Chicago, IL 60611
(312) 337-1000
www.jameshotels.com/chicago

Michigan Avenue shopping? Millennium Park? Museums? If you plan to do it all, the James Hotel is a great choice. This boutique hotel has a wide range of room choices—regular guestrooms, studios, lofts, one-bedroom apartments, and penthouse lofts—and the on-site David Burke's Primehouse offers 24-hour room service so you can enjoy a scrumptious meal right in your room.

Families can book the Lil' James Family Adventurer Package, which includes a welcome amenity for kids, milk and cookies turndown treat, and the Lil' James amenity program offering access to in-room DVDs, maps, and guides to Chicago. Bikes are available for use for both kids and adults in case you want to explore the city on two wheels.

The James Hotel is a four-star hotel with lots of lovely extras, like eco-friendly pillow options, triple-filtered water in rooms, a fitness center, and spa services. Best of all, you can make the most of every hour because check-in is at 2:00 p.m. and check-out is also at 2:00 p.m. Even the furry little ones will love it: pet amenities include plush beds, leather leashes and collars, and treats.

Rates start at about $185 a night.

Take the Red Line train to 95th or Howard and get off at Grand. Walk north toward Ontario and turn right.

Parking: $65 valet parking with in and out privileges.

THE LANGHAM CHICAGO

30 N. Wabash Avenue, Chicago, IL 60611
(312) 923-9988
langhamhotels.com

Parents, hold on to your hats—the five-star Langham Chicago has a kids' play room with video games, board games, musical instruments, AND a 12-seat cinema showing movies for kids. Impressive, huh? That's not all, because they also provide in-town car service within two miles of the hotel and have a spa, fitness center, and pool. The little details add up to make the accommodations at The

Langham Chicago luxurious, like floor-to-ceiling windows for amazing views of the city and sparkly lights above the swimming pool.

Both rooms and suites are available. Travelle restaurant is located at The Langham, and they also have Langham Afternoon Tea with Wedgewood in the elegant Pavilion.

Rates start at about $315 a night.

CTA bus routes #29, #36, and #62 stop at State and Marina City, just outside the hotel. The CTA trains from the Brown, Orange, Purple, Green, and Pink lines stop at State and Lake, a few blocks away.

Valet parking is available for about $70 a night.

LOEWS CHICAGO HOTEL
455 N. Park Drive, Chicago, IL 60611
(312) 840-6600
www.loewshotels.com/chicago-downtown

Being "Snowed Inn" has never been as fun as it is at Loews Chicago Hotel. With this special package, guests get hot chocolate and cookies, a free in-room movie, and a children's pop-up tent and campfire set for the kids to use during their stay. This is just one of the packages offered for families. Loews also has a Loews Loves Kids program that provides families with things they may need (or want) during their stay, such as childproofing kits, access to a lending library, and a "kids closet" with toys and strollers. They also offer iPads, PlayStation consoles, and Xbox systems for use by tweens and teens. Even the furry family members are included, with the Loews Loves Pets program offering the use of leashes, collars, and treats during your stay.

Loews has luxury rooms and suites, complete with a Keurig coffeemaker, free wifi, and 24-hour room service. The Loews car service can take you to your destination within two miles of the hotel, and—considering Loews' prime location—that two miles covers many of the major attractions in Chicago. Rural Society, an Argentinian steakhouse, is on the premises, and Loews also has a spa with services available for relaxation and rejuvenation. Need a night off? Babysitters are available!

Rates start at about $170 a night.

CTA bus routes #66 and #124 stop on Columbus at North Water Street.

Self-parking is about $40; **valet parking** is about $70.

OMNI CHICAGO HOTEL

676 N. Michigan Avenue, Chicago, IL 60611
(312) 944-6664
https://www.omnihotels.com/hotels/chicago

Lavish is the only way to describe the Omni Chicago Hotel, the only all-suite hotel on Chicago's Michigan Avenue. Each suite has a wet bar, and refrigerators are available by request. If you need an extra bed, Omni has rollaway beds and cribs available at no charge. Numerous awesome Chicago attractions are within just a couple miles of the Omni, and some are only a few blocks away.

The Omni Kids Crew provides kids with a backpack filled with fun items upon check-in, as well as milk and cookies. Omni has an indoor pool, two rooftop sundecks, a fitness center, and the 676 Restaurant. Omni knows how important safety is to parents, so they have outlet covers available, as well as first aid kits. When you're booking, check out their special offers for a variety of American Girl packages and other delightful packages; you can even customize your stay with the Build Your Own Package, in which you can choose what perks you'd like to receive at a discount.

Rates start at about $130 a night.

Multiple CTA bus routes stop on Michigan at Ohio and at Superior.
The CTA Red Line train stops at Chicago on State Street about half a mile away.

Valet parking is about $70 a night.

RAFFAELLO HOTEL

201 E. Delaware Place, Chicago, IL 60611
(312) 943-5000
http://www.chicagoraffaello.com

The Raffaello is a four-star boutique hotel in the Gold Coast, conveniently located near the John Hancock Center, the Magnificent Mile, and the Museum of Contemporary Art. On-site is Drumbar, a rooftop bar, and Pelago Ristorante, an upscale Italian restaurant. Although neither of these is child-friendly, they're a nice getaway for parents who have childcare options. Room service is available, and parents and kids will love Glazed & Infused, the small shop in the lobby offering coffee and artisan donuts. There's no shortage of dining options in the area—everything from fast food to Chicago favorites like Gino's East.

All rooms have Keurig coffeemakers, a mini-fridge, and microwave, which is not only convenient, but helpful if you want to save a few bucks by making coffee or food in your room. King and double rooms are available, as well as Deluxe and Grand Suites. The suites are particularly nice for families with young children as they have a separate bedroom with doors. Raffaello offers discounts on multi-night stays and seasonal deals and packages.

Rates start at about $200 a night.

Blocks away from Chestnut and Mies van der Rohe bus stop and DeWitt and Chestnut bus stop. About half a mile from the Chicago stop on the CTA Red Line.

Parking lot and **valet parking** are available. There are several parking garages in the area.

THE RITZ-CARLTON

Water Tower Place, 160 E. Pearson Street, Chicago, IL 60611
(312) 266-1000
http://www.ritzcarlton.com/en/hotels/chicago

It goes without saying that the five-star Ritz-Carlton is going to be pretty impressive. The lobby of the hotel, located on the twelfth floor, contains an elaborate fountain, a giant skylight, and comfortable seating with amazing views of the city. Across the street is the Museum of Contemporary Art and a park and playground for when you want to enjoy the fresh air or let the kids burn off some energy. Deca, the roof-top restaurant, offers breakfast, lunch, and dinner dishes made from fresh, local ingredients, and they have a kids' menu.

Located at the top of Water Tower Place, the Ritz-Carlton provides indulgent accommodations and services for all its guests, including children. They have an indoor pool and fitness center, and they offer yoga, Pilates, and water aerobics classes; even kids can get active with a Zumba kids class. Young visitors can participate in cupcake decorating (complete with chef's hat) with the pastry chef, and the "Candy Man" can come to your room with a cart full of treats. Book the "Fido's Family Getaway" and kids get a tent in the room, popcorn, a DVD to watch, and they can choose a toy from the Red Wagon while your canine family member is pampered with a doggy bed and special gourmet doggy treat at turndown.

Rates start at about $330 a night.
Multiple CTA buses make stops along Michigan Avenue and Chestnut Street.
Valet parking is about $70 per day.

SWISSOTEL

323 E. Upper Wacker Drive, Chicago, IL 60601
(312) 565 0565
www.swissotel.com/hotels/chicago

The exterior of the Swissotel is sure to catch your eye—it's an all-glass triangular building. Inside, be ready to indulge. This four-star hotel is pet-friendly and offers an indoor pool and two restaurants. The Geneva Restaurant is open for breakfast only and serves classic American breakfast food with a hint of European style. The Palm, open for lunch and dinner, serves American and Italian food and has caricatures of local celebrities on the walls. Book a Swissotel Kids Suite package for accommodations in a two-room suite with toys, books, and games, plus complimentary breakfast and tickets to either the Field Museum or the Shedd Aquarium.

During the holiday season, Swissotel has a Santa Suite decorated especially for the big guy, with free elf-led tours for guests and the public, including special activities like a letter-writing station and visits from Santa himself.

Rates start at about $100.
CTA bus routes #6, #20, #124, #134, #135, and #136 stop on Columbus at East Wacker.
Self-parking is about $40; **valet** is about $70.

⁎ OUTSKIRTS OF CHICAGO ⁎

Staying in the downtown area has a few drawbacks. First of all, it can be pretty pricey. In addition to the cost of your stay, most downtown hotels also charge for parking, which can be $30 to $70 (or even more) a day. Some offer in-and-out privileges, while others charge a separate fee each time you park your car.

Also, while many Chicago hotels offer first-class family amenities (often at additional cost), there are common amenities families often look for that might be a little harder to find in the city—like free parking, complimentary breakfast, or an indoor pool.

Finally, if room size is important, you may want to think twice about downtown hotels. Rooms in the city hotels tend to be smaller. There are definitely large rooms available, but they'll be more expensive. If you're spending your whole trip exploring, a small room might be perfectly fine, but some families might prefer to get more space for their buck outside the city limits.

If downtown Chicago hotels just aren't in your budget or don't have the amenities you're looking for, there are plenty of other options. Here are a few places you can stay instead:

Midway Airport

Midway Airport is on the southwest side of the city in a residential area. A couple miles south of the airport is the Midway Hotel Center, a group of ten chain hotels, and there are additional hotels in the area as well. While the airport and Midway Hotel Center are inside the city of Chicago, it's just on the border of the suburbs. You won't get breathtaking views or world-class attractions within walking distance, but restaurants and stores are nearby, the prices are not as high as in the downtown area of the city, and parking is often free. The CTA Orange Line station is near the airport, and the expressway is just a couple miles south of the hotels. The south and west suburbs are each a short drive away or can be reached by train.

Here are some places with family-friendly features in the Midway Airport area:

- **Best Western Inn & Suites—Midway Airport**
  8220 S. Cicero, Burbank, IL 60459
  (708) 497-3000
  http://www.bestwesternmidway.com/
  Two-star hotel. Free parking, wifi, and breakfast. Indoor pool. Suites available.
  Rates start at about $90.

- **Carlton Inn Midway**
  4944 S. Archer Avenue, Chicago, IL 60632
  (855) 213-0582
  http://www.carltoninnmidway.com/
  Two-star hotel. Free wifi, airport shuttle, parking, and breakfast. Pets allowed.
  Rates start at about $130.

- **Fairfield Inn & Suites Chicago Midway Airport**
  6630 S. Cicero Avenue, Bedford Park, IL 60638
  (708) 594-0090
  http://www.marriott.com/hotels/travel/chimd-fairfield-inn-and-suites-chicago-midway-airport/
  Two-star hotel. Free wifi, breakfast. Indoor pool, room service. Suites available.
  Rates start at about $170. $17 for parking.

- **Holiday Inn Chicago—Midway Airport**
  6624 S. Cicero Avenue, Chicago, IL 60638
  (708) 563-6490
  http://www.midwayhotelcenter.com/holiday-inn-chicago-midway-airport.htm
  Three-star hotel. Free shuttle. Coaches Sports Bar, Kids Eat Free Program, indoor pool, room service. Connecting rooms available.
  Rates start at about $190.

- **Hyatt Place Chicago Midway Airport**
  6550 S. Cicero Avenue, Chicago, IL 60638
  (708) 594-1400
  http://www.chicagomidwayairport.place.hyatt.com/en/hotel/home.html
  Three star hotel. Free wifi, parking, shuttle, and breakfast. Indoor pool. Suites available.
  Rates start at about $170.

- **Quality Inn Midway Airport**
  7353 S. Cicero Avenue, Chicago, IL 60629
  (773) 581-5300
  https://www.choicehotels.com/illinois/chicago/quality-inn-hotels/il384?source=gyxt
  Two-year hotel. Free wifi, airport shuttle, and parking.
  Rates start at about $110.

O'Hare Airport

On the far northwest side of the city is O'Hare Airport. While the airport is technically in Chicago (thanks to some bizarre angles and extensions to the border), it's surrounded by suburbs, so hotels in this area are in Rosemont, Des Plaines, and Schiller Park. You'll find several restaurants and shopping plazas nearby, and you can check out the West suburbs section for things to do in the area. O'Hare Airport is about a 45-minute drive from downtown Chicago.

- **Candlewood Suites Chicago-O'Hare**
  4021 Mannheim Road, Schiller Park, IL 60176
  (847) 671-4663
  https://www.ihg.com/candlewood/hotels/us/en/schiller-park/chimr/
  hoteldetail?cm_mmc=GoogleMaps-_-CW-_-USA-_-CHIMR
  Two-star hotel. Free parking, free wifi, pets allowed, free shuttle, lending library, and lending locker.
  Rates start at about $90.

- **Courtyard Chicago O'Hare**
  2950 S. River Road, Des Plaines, IL 60018
  (847) 824-7000
  http://www.marriott.com/hotels/travel/chica-courtyard-chicago-ohare/?scid=bb1a189a-fec3-4d19-a255-54ba596febe2
  Three-star hotel. Suites available. Free wifi, restaurant on-site, indoor pool.
  Rates start at about $190.

- **Hampton Inn Chicago-O'Hare International Airport**
  3939 N. Mannheim Road, Schiller Park, IL 60176
  (847) 671-1700
  http://hamptoninn3.hilton.com/en/hotels/illinois/hampton-inn-chicago-ohare-international-airport-CHIAPHX/index.html
  Three-star hotel. Suites available, free wifi, free breakfast, indoor pool.
  Rates start at about $115.

- **Hampton Inn & Suites Rosemont Chicago O'Hare**
  9480 W. Higgins Road, Rosemont, IL 60018
  (847) 692-3000
  http://hamptoninn3.hilton.com/en/hotels/illinois/hampton-inn-and-suites rosemont-chicago-ohare-CHIRSHX/index.html
  Three-star hotel. Free wifi, free shuttle, free breakfast, indoor pool.
  Rates start at about $115.

- **Hilton Garden Inn Chicago O'Hare Airport**
  2930 S. River Road, Des Plaines, IL 60018
  (847) 296-8900

http://hiltongardeninn3.hilton.com/en/hotels/illinois/hilton-garden-inn-chicago-ohare-airport-ORDCHGI/index.html

Three-star hotel. Free wifi, indoor pool, complimentary shuttle, restaurant on-site, microwave and refrigerator in rooms.

Rates start at about $130.

- **Sheraton Chicago O'Hare**
  6501 Mannheim Road, Rosemont, IL 60018
  (847) 699-6300
  http://www.sheratonchicagoohare.com/
  Four-star hotel. All suites, complimentary shuttle, pets allowed, restaurant on-site, and room service available.
  Rates start at about $160.

Brookfield/Oak Park/Oak Brook

The Western suburbs—including Brookfield, Oak Park, and Oak Brook—offer many benefits to traveling families. Brookfield Zoo is just one popular Chicago attraction located in this area; LaGrange is nearby as well, a suburb with a small town feel that's a great place to explore. Visitors who stay here will find reasonably priced rooms with free parking, convenient shopping and restaurants, and it's close to expressways. Travel during non-rush hours and it'll only take about 20 to 30 minutes to reach downtown Chicago. Oak Park has countless restaurants and boutique shops and is popular among families, while Oak Brook is a bustling shopping area with miles of popular stores and restaurants and a large outdoor mall.

- **Best Western Chicagoland—Countryside**
  6251 Joliet Street, Countryside, IL 60525
  (708) 354-5200
  http://bestwesternillinois.com/hotels/best-western-chicagoland-countryside
  Three-star hotel. Free parking, free breakfast, free wifi, microwave and refrigerator in each room.
  Rates start at about $100.

- **The Carleton of Oak Park**
  1110 Pleasant Street, Oak Park, IL 60302
  (708) 848-5000
  www.carletonhotel.com
  Three-star hotel. Suites available, free wifi, free parking, restaurant on-site, all rooms have a microwave and refrigerator.
  Rates start at about $165.

- **Hyatt Place Chicago/Lombard/Oak Brook**
  2340 S. Fountain Square Drive, Lombard, IL 60148
  (630) 932-6501
  www.lombard.place.hyatt.com/en/hotel/home.html
  Three-star hotel. Free parking, free wifi, free breakfast, complimentary shuttle, indoor pool.
  Rates start at about $140.

- **Hilton Chicago Oak Brook Hills Resort & Conference Center**
  3500 Midwest Road, Oak Brook, IL 60523
  (630) 850-5555
  http://www3.hilton.com/en/hotels/illinois/hilton-chicago-oak-brook-hills-resort-and-conference-center-CHIBHHH/index.html
  Four-star resort. Suites available, free parking, restaurant on-site, bike rentals, indoor and outdoor pools, pets allowed, complimentary shuttle, and 18-hole golf course.
  Rates start at about $130.

- **Hilton Chicago/Oak Brook Suites**
  10 Drury Lane, Oakbrook Terrace, IL 60181
  (630) 941-0100
  http://www3.hilton.com/en/hotels/illinois/hilton-chicago-oak-brook-suites-CHIOTHS/index.html
  Three-star hotel. Suites available, free parking, restaurant on-site, room service available, indoor pool.
  Rates start at about $145.

- **Residence Inn Chicago Oak Brook**
  790 Jorie Boulevard, Oak Brook, IL 60523
  (630) 571-1200
  www.marriott.com/hotels/travel/chibk-residence-inn-chicago-oak-brook/
  Four-star hotel. All suites, full kitchens, free parking, free wifi, indoor pool, free breakfast.
  Rates start at about $135.

Schaumburg

Schaumburg is a large suburb about 30 miles west of Chicago, and it's a big shopping destination with one large mall, many strip malls and specialty shops, and Ikea. Rooms in Schaumburg aren't very expensive, and you can find hotels with family suites for about what you'd pay for a single room in the city. Restaurants are plentiful and there are several attractions, including LEGOLAND Discovery Center, Medieval Times, Schaumburg Boomers, and Level 257.

- **Chicago Marriott Schaumburg**
  50 N. Martingale Road, Schaumburg, IL 60173
  (847) 240-0100
  http://www.marriott.com/hotels/travel/chisb-chicago-marriott-schaumburg/
  Three-star hotel. Free parking, indoor and outdoor pool, and restaurant.
  Rates start at about $150.

- **Comfort Suites**
  1100 E. Higgins Road, Schaumburg, IL 60173
  (847) 330-0133
  https://www.choicehotels.com/illinois/schaumburg/comfort-suites-hotels/
  Two-star hotel. Free wifi and breakfast, restaurant, indoor pool, and kitchens in suites.
  Rates start at about $80.

- **Eaglewood Resort and Spa**
  1401 Nordic Road, Itasca, IL 60143
  (630) (773) 1400
  http://www.eaglewoodresort.com/
  Four-star resort. Free wifi, indoor pool, restaurant, and spa.
  Rates start at about $150.

- **Homewood Suites Chicago-Schaumburg**
  815 American Lane, Schaumburg, IL 60173
  (847) 605-0400
  http://homewoodsuites3.hilton.com/en/hotels/illinois/homewood-suites-by-hilton-chicago-schaumburg-CHISMHW/index.html
  Three-star hotel. Free parking, wifi, and breakfast, outdoor pool, pets allowed, and kitchens in suites.
  Rates start at about $120.

- **Hilton Indian Lakes Resort**
  250 W. Schick Road, Bloomingdale, IL 60108
  (630) 529-0200
  http://www3.hilton.com/en/hotels/illinois/hilton-chicago-indian-lakes-resort-ORDILHF/index.html
  Three-star resort. Free parking and wifi, indoor and outdoor pool, restaurant, and spa.
  Rates start at about $100

- **Renaissance Schaumburg Convention Center Hotel**
  1551 Thoreau Drive N., Schaumburg, IL 60173
  (847) 303-4100
  http://www.marriott.com/hotels/travel/chirs-renaissance-schaumburg-convention-center-hotel/
  Four-star hotel. Free parking, indoor pool, and restaurant.
  Rates start at about $160.

- **Springhill Suites Chicago Schaumburg**
  1550 McConnor Parkway, Schaumburg, IL 60173
  (847) 995-1500
  http://www.marriott.com/hotels/travel/chisg-springhill-suites-chicago-
  schaumburg-woodfield-mall
  Three-star hotel. Free parking, wifi, and breakfast; indoor pool and spa.
  Rates start at about $80.

North Suburbs

Head north on I-94 and you'll wind up in the north suburbs—Glenview, Northbrook, and Lincolnshire, just to name a few. This is a great place to do a little
sight-seeing while you drive because there are some really beautiful (and huge)
homes in these suburbs. Writer, director, and producer John Hughes lived in
Northbrook and subsequently used this area to film lots of famous scenes from
his movies, including the house from *Home Alone*, Cameron's house and the
high school from *Ferris Bueller's Day Off*, and the church from *Sixteen Candles*.
The Chicago Botanic Garden, Funtopia, the Kohl Children's Museum, and the
Marriott Theatre are in the area, and there are plenty of restaurants.

- **Best Western Plus Glenview-Chicagoland Inn & Suites**
  4514 W. Lake Avenue, Glenview, IL 60026
  (847) 635-5220
  https://www.bestwestern.com/en_US/book/hotels-in-glenview/best-western-
  plus-glenview-chicagoland-inn-suites/propertyCode.14201.html
  Three-star hotel. Free parking, wifi, and breakfast; outdoor pool, fitness
  center.
  Rates start at about $90.

- **Extended Stay America Chicago-Vernon Hills-Lincolnshire**
  675 Woodlands Parkway, Vernon Hills, IL 60061
  (847) 955-1111
  http://www.extendedstayamerica.com/hotels/il/chicago/vernon-hills-
  lincolnshire
  Two-star hotel. Free parking and breakfast, full kitchens in suites, and pet-
  friendly.
  Rates start at about $70.

- **Hampton Inn & Suites Chicago-North Shore-Skokie**
  5201 Old Orchard Road, Skokie, IL 60077
  (847) 583-1111
  http://hamptoninn3.hilton.com/en/hotels/illinois/hampton-inn-and-suites-
  chicago-north-shore-skokie-CHISKHX/index.html

- **Three-star hotel.** Free parking, wifi, and breakfast; indoor pool, fitness center, refrigerator and microwave in rooms.
  Rates start at about $115.

- **Lincolnshire Marriott Resort**
  10 Marriott Drive, Lincolnshire, IL 60069
  (847) 634-0100
  http://www.marriott.com/hotels/travel/chiln-lincolnshire-marriott-resort/
  Four-star resort. Free parking, indoor pool, restaurant, indoor and outdoor pool, fitness center.
  Rates start at about $190.

- **Residence Inn Chicago Wilmette/Skokie**
  3205 Old Glenview Road, Wilmette, IL 60091
  (847) 251-6600
  http://www.marriott.com/hotels/travel/chiwl-residence-inn-chicago-wilmette-skokie/
  Three-star hotel. Free parking, wifi, and breakfast; indoor pool, pet-friendly, kitchens in all rooms.
  Rates start at about $110.

- **SpringHill Suites Chicago Lincolnshire**
  300 Marriott Drive, Lincolnshire, IL 60069
  (847) 793-7500
  http://www.marriott.com/hotels/travel/chish-springhill-suites-chicago-lincolnshire/
  Three-star hotel. Free parking, wifi, and breakfast; indoor pool, fitness center, kitchenette in all rooms.
  Rates start at about $110 a night.

Additional Places to Stay

There are a few other places that don't fit in the above-listed categories, but they're great places for families to stay and are worth considering.

PHEASANT RUN RESORT
4051 East Main Street, St. Charles, IL 60174
(630) 584-6300
http://www.pheasantrun.com/

St. Charles is a western suburb about 40 miles outside of Chicago with lots of small-town charm, shopping, dining, and a riverwalk along the Fox River. It's also the home to the Pheasant Run Resort. Offering single rooms with a view of the golf course or from the tower and bi-level apartment-style suites, Pheasant Run can easily accommodate families of various sizes.

On the resort property, you'll find an 18-hole golf course, six restaurants, indoor and outdoor pools, a fitness center, Spa Vargas, and two entertainment venues—Zanies Comedy Club and Jambalaya, with a DJ or live band. The Pheasant Run KidsKlub offers special activities and crafts for kids on weekends. Pheasant Run offers many packages and specials, including the Family Fun package with breakfast and a pizza dinner from room service along with your room.

Rates start at about $95 a night.
Public transportation is not available nearby.
Free parking in lot.

CYPRESS RESORT AND MARINA
25635 W. Hermann Avenue, Antioch, IL 60002
(224) 381-3960
http://www.cypressofantioch.com/
Open year-round

When summer arrives it's time to head for the beach, and Cypress Resort and Marina will make you feel like you're hundreds of miles away from the hectic city when it's actually only about 60 miles from the center of Chicago. The resort has been owned by the same family since the 1980s and was recently rehabbed and reopened. Located on Petite Lake, the 20-acre Cypress Resort is made up of the Boat House (which can be rented out for weddings or other special events), a marina, and ten cottages. The cottages vary in size and capacity, but the largest sleeps eight people. Each cottage is unique, with charming décor, lots of character, and a kitchen so you can make your own meals if you'd like. Kitchen essentials are included, and wifi is available, but there are no televisions, so plan on spending some quality family time together and getting outdoors! The Cypress Resort marina is private and gated with 20 boat slips, 480 feet of sandy beach, a picnic area with grills, and bathrooms with showers. Guests of the resort have access to kayaks, paddleboats, a rowboat, life vests, and floaties for fun in the water.

There are plenty of restaurants not far from the resort, and if you're looking for a little more excitement during your stay, Six Flags Great America is about a half-hour drive away. Cypress Resort is open year-round, so don't let cold weather keep you away!

Rates start at about $125 a night.
There is no public transportation available nearby.
Free parking.

ILLINOIS BEACH RESORT AND CONFERENCE CENTER
1 Lake Front Drive, Zion, IL 60099
(847) 625-7300
www.ilresorts.com

Illinois Beach Resort and Conference Center is right in the middle between Chicago and Milwaukee; about a 40-minute drive from each. This three-star resort sits right on Lake Michigan, so visitors have great views and use of the beach right outside their door. Free wifi, a large indoor pool, a fitness center, a game room, and the spacious lawn make this a great spot for families to enjoy some time away. Six Flags Great America is a 30-minute drive, and the Gurnee Mills Shopping Center is just 20 minutes away. The Lakeside Restaurant serves up prime rib, Atlantic cod, children's favorites, and beautiful views from the dining room.

Moms, dads, and teens might enjoy golfing on one of the two nearby courses, fishing expeditions available nearby, or the massage services at the resort. Illinois Beach Resort has a variety of booking packages available including a Family Vacation package that includes a pizza dinner and a Six Flags Great America package.

Rates start at about $100 a night.

The closest public transportation is about a mile and a half away; the Pace bus route #571 stops at Sheridan/Wadsworth.

Parking in the lot is free.

THINGS TO DO
BY REGION

DOWNTOWN CHICAGO/LOOP

This is where the action is. The "Loop" is the business district of Chicago, and many say the name originally comes from the route of streetcars in the 1800s, which formed a loop in this area, and today the "L" trains form a loop as well.

Skyscrapers, luxury shopping and dining, and many iconic Chicago attractions can be found in the downtown Loop area. World-famous museums, parks, and outdoor sculptures ensure a grand experience whether you're looking to spend a lot, a little, or nothing at all.

Attractions

360 CHICAGO AT THE JOHN HANCOCK BUILDING
875 N. Michigan Avenue, 94th floor, Chicago, IL 60611
(888) 875-8439
www.360Chicago.com
Open 9:00 a.m.–11:00 p.m. 365 days a year.

Picture this: You're enjoying the view of the city from 1,000 feet up when suddenly the window begins to tilt out, and you go along with it, leaning over Michigan Avenue. Scary? Exhilarating? Try it to find out. Tilt at 360 Chicago allows eight adventurers to tilt 30 degrees over the street for a unique view. It's an additional $7, but well worth it (I'm told).

If you're brave enough to try it (or just want to watch others do it), you'll find Tilt on the 94th floor of the John Hancock Center. Hop on the fastest elevators in North America, which will take you to the 94th floor at a rate of 25 feet per second. Once you're up there, 360 Chicago offers some amazing views, as well as the Architect's Corner café, a gift shop, and a kiosk where you can make your own free e-postcard. Interactive technology and panoramic touch screens provide information and entertainment for children and adults. On special activity nights, you can experience free guided tours, listen to live music, paint, or set up a tripod for photos.

Insider tip: Bring some gum for yourself and the kids (or sippy cups for babies or toddlers) because it will help ears pop comfortably during the elevator ride.

General admission is $20 for adults, $13 for children ages 3–11. Chicago residents get 50% off general admission prices. The Tilt experience is an additional $7.

Good for all ages.

Time to explore: 1–2 hours

CTA #125 Water Tower Express bus stops at the John Hancock Building.

Parking at the John Hancock Center garage is about $35.

ADLER PLANETARIUM

1300 S. Lake Shore Drive, Chicago, IL 60605
(312) 922-7827
www.adlerplanetarium.org
Open 9:30 a.m.–4:00 p.m. Monday through Friday,
9:30 a.m.–4:30 p.m. Saturday and Sunday.

Take a trip out of this world at the Adler Planetarium, where visitors can learn the secrets of the Universe, from the technology behind telescopes, to the evolution of the Universe from the Big Bang to modern day, to the Moon mission. Young visitors (ages 3–8) will love the Planet Explorers area where they can be scientists and astronauts while launching rockets, searching for signs of life on Planet X, and operating the controls in the two-story rocket. Of course, there are opportunities to climb and play too.

Although not included in general admission, the Adler Planetarium offers a variety of sky shows in their three theaters that are well worth the extra expense. These are more than just shows, they're experiences, thanks to the 3-D capabilities in the Johnson Star Theater and the immersive domed Grainger Sky and Definiti Space Theaters. There are several different shows, including one for the littlest kids, *One World, One Sky: Big Bird's Adventure*, which shows how, despite geographical distances on Earth, we all see the same night sky.

The Adler Planetarium has plenty of special events, including Sun Salutations yoga classes in the Grainger Sky Theater (ages 10 and up) and observation parties for eclipses and other astronomical events, so be sure to check their calendar.

Insider tip: Save Planet Explorers for last. The kids will love it, and it'll be hard to drag them out of there to see other exhibits if you go there first.

General admission is $12 for adults, $8 for children ages 3–11. All-access passes cost about $30–$35 and include shows, all exhibitions, and the Atwood Sphere Experience.

Best for ages 3 and up.

Time to explore: 3–4 hours

Bus #146 to the Inner Drive/Museum Campus stop takes you to the planetarium. The #130 bus also goes to the Museum Campus, but only in the summer. The CTA Red, Orange, and Green lines go to Roosevelt stop.

A limited amount of metered parking is available near the museum. The Museum Campus parking lot is $20, but the price varies during sporting events or special events in the area.

AMERICAN GIRL PLACE

835 N. Michigan Avenue, Chicago, IL 60611
(877) 247-5223
http://www.americangirl.com/retailstore/chicago
Saturday 9:00 a.m.–9:00 p.m., Sunday 9:00 a.m.–6:00 p.m., Monday–Thursday
10:00 a.m.–8:00 p.m.

Chicago is home to the first—and one of the largest—American Girl Place stores in the world. It sits in the northeast corner of Water Tower Place, and it is enormous. Near the main entrance, you'll be greeted by displays of many of the new dolls, their outfits and accessories, and a bookstore of American Girl titles. The first story also has the American Girl BeForever dolls and the merchandise that goes with them; there are detailed displays and a large collection of matching and coordinating outfits for girls and their dolls. The American Girl Place carries a collection of Truly Me dolls, so girls can choose a doll that resembles them, as well as Bitty Baby and Bitty Twins dolls for younger children.

Of course, it's not just about shopping for dolls at American Girl Place, it's about the experience. Dolls for younger kids are in a nursery area where they can choose a doll and then bathe them, clothe them, and choose infant accessories. Girls and their dolls (and families) can dine at the ultra-pink café upstairs, create personalized clothing, get a new hairstyle at the salon (sorry—dolls only), and enjoy a pastry at the "sidewalk" café.

Insider tip: Many Chicago hotels partner with American Girl Place to offer special packages that include overnight accommodations and a shopping experience.

Free to browse. Dolls start at about $60.

Best for ages 3–12 years old.

Time to explore: 1–3 hours

Standard parking garage at 111 E. Chestnut (entrance on East Peterson) offers discounted parking rates with a purchase.

Buses stop at nearby Chestnut and Mies van der Rohe and at Michigan and Chestnut.

ART INSTITUTE OF CHICAGO

111 S. Michigan Avenue, Chicago, IL 60603
(312) 433-3600
www.artic.edu
Open 10:30 a.m.–5:00 p.m. daily and until 8:00 p.m. on Thursdays.

The Art Institute is the second-largest art museum in the country, with about a million square feet, but that shouldn't scare you off—this is still a great family destination. They have monthly stroller tours (reservations required) and host-themed Family Festivals, and the museum café has a kids' menu.

The Art Institute has a wide range of exhibits, such as textiles, architecture and design, Medieval and Renaissance works, and arms and armor. You'll see price-less masterpieces here, like Vincent van Gogh's *Self Portrait*, Edward Hopper's *Nighthawks*, Claude Monet's *Waterlilies*, and Grant Wood's *American Gothic*. Georges-Pierre Seurat's *Sunday Afternoon on the Island of La Grande Jatte* is on display at the Art Institute, and it's amazing to see the tiny little details on such a huge canvas. (Plus, if you want a playful, uniquely Chicago souvenir, snap a photo of family members in front of it à la *Ferris Bueller's Day Off*.)

Peeking into the Thorne Miniature Rooms is always a magical experience, and even more so in November and December when they are decorated for the holidays. Thanks to steps in front of the displays, smaller children will have no problem peering in by themselves.

Insider tip: The Artist's Studio in the Ryan Learning Center has drop-in projects for kids and parents to do every day from 10:30 a.m. to 5:00 p.m. Activities/themes are linked to current exhibits.

General admission is $25 for adults and $19 for students and teens 14–17. Children under 14 are free. Chicago residents receive a $5 discount, and Illinois residents receive a $3 discount on tickets. A fast pass is available for $35. Illinois residents receive free admission 5:00 p.m.–8:00 p.m. on Thursdays.

Best for grade schoolers and up.

Time to explore: 2–3 hours

Brown, Green, Orange, Pink, and Purple lines stop at Adams/Wabash, one block away. The Blue Line stops underground at Monroe. Multiple buses stop within a few blocks of the museum.

Valet parking is available for about $30 (cash only). There are parking lots available near Millennium Park.

CHICAGO ARCHITECTURE FOUNDATION

224 S. Michigan Avenue, Chicago, IL 60604
(312) 922-3432
http://www.architecture.org/
9:30 a.m.–6:30 p.m. daily

The Chicago Architecture Foundation is a non-profit organization dedicated to inspiring people to discover why design matters. Approximately 1,000 volunteers work with the CAF to share information and a love of architecture and design with all who are interested.

The Chicago Model—a 3-D model depicting 400 blocks of Chicago buildings—is on permanent display at the Michigan Avenue location, and they also have temporary exhibits and a gift shop. Visit between noon and 5:00 p.m. to participate in their open Design Studio, which gives visitors a hands-on experience. The Chicago Architecture Foundation hosts classes, camps, and workshops for children and families, so be sure to check out their schedule; many activities are free!

The CAF offers an assortment of tours throughout the city; prices range from about $16 to $45 for a tour, and they offer tours taken on foot, by boat, on bike or Segway, by bus or trolley, and even on the L train.

Insider tip: The Chicago Architecture Foundation's tours don't stop at the city limits; check out their tour schedule and you'll find tours of the suburbs as well as downtown and Chicago neighborhoods.

Free to visit; architecture tours vary in price.

Good for all ages.

Tours vary from 1 to 4 hours.

Multiple buses stop at Michigan and Jackson and the Brown, Orange, Green, Pink, and Purple lines stop at Adams and Wabash.

Millennium Park Garage/Grant Park South are both nearby, and parking is usually $30–$35.

CHICAGO CHILDREN'S MUSEUM

700 E. Grand Avenue, Chicago, IL 60611
(312) 527-1000
www.chicagochildrensmuseum.org
Open 10:00 a.m.–5:00 p.m. Sunday through Wednesday, 5:00 p.m.–8:00 p.m. Thursday, 10:00 a.m. (9:00 a.m. for members)–6:00 p.m. Friday and Saturday.

Kids can spend the day splashing in the water table, donning some firefighter gear, digging for dinosaurs, or building their own skyscraper at the Chicago Children's Museum, which houses three floors of fun.

Babies, toddlers, and preschoolers can have an outdoor adventure indoors in the Treehouse Trails exhibit; repair a car, drive a CTA bus, or shop at the grocery store in the Kids Town exhibit. Or they can attend a daily open play group in the Pritzker Playspace. All these areas are gated to help keep little ones from getting away from parents.

Treasure hunt anyone? Michael's Museum, a room filled with over 100 collections of tiny items, has plenty to explore, from a tiny mouse hole near the entrance to drawers and drawers of little surprises. Grab a laminated card and hunt for the items on the card. Older kids will love the Tinkering Lab, where they can use real tools to build and create.

For kids old enough the climb it (generally age 5 and up), the highlight of the trip will likely be the three-story schooner. Rope ladders and wooden bridges run from the first-floor "cargo hold" to the third-floor ship's top. Before leaving the museum be sure to stop at the Story Hub, where the kids (or the whole family) can make a movie about their experience at the museum. Videos can be viewed online after you go home.

Insider tip: Make sure to leave extra time when you visit the Chicago Children's Museum; its location at Navy Pier means there's lots more to do, so plan to spend the day at the Pier.

$14 per person; children under age 1 are free. Free admission on Thursday evenings and on the first Sunday of each month.

Best for kids ages 10 and under.

Time to explore: 3–4 hours

CTA bus routes #29 State Street, #65 Grand Avenue, #66 Chicago Avenue, and #124 Navy Pier Express (serving METRA lines, Millennium Park/Randolph St., Ogilvie and Union Stations) will take you to Navy Pier. The #2 Hyde Park Express also serves Navy Pier.

Parking in the Navy Pier parking garages is $25. If they are full, you can also park at Grand Plaza Park (540 N. State) or Ogden Plaza Self Park (300 E. North Water Street) for $15 with validation from Navy Pier; both are less than half a mile away, and you can walk or take a trolley (seasonally) to Navy Pier.

BUCKINGHAM FOUNTAIN

301 S. Columbus Drive, Chicago, IL 60605
(312) 742-7259
http://www.chicagoparkdistrict.com/parks/clarence-f-buckingham-memorial-fountain/
8:00 a.m.–11:00 p.m. daily from April until mid-October

Buckingham Fountain is nearly a century old and can be found in historic Grant Park, along Lake Shore Drive across from the Chicago Harbor. Grant Park is the center of the city, with plenty of open space for walking and enjoying the scenery and a plethora of attractions within walking distance. Add Buckingham Fountain to your itinerary when you're visiting the Art Institute, Millennium Park, the Shedd Aquarium, Field Museum, or Adler Planetarium. Synchronized water displays run for 20 minutes every hour, with water shooting up to 150 feet into the air. After dusk, the display becomes even more impressive with a light show and musical accompaniment.

Tip: Visit after dusk. The light, music, and water show is a perfect way to end a summer evening.

Free

Good for all ages.

Time to explore: 1 hour or less

Some metered street parking available nearby; parking garages nearby also.

Balbo and Columbus bus stop is nearby, or take the ME or SS train to Van Buren Street.

FEDERAL RESERVE BANK OF CHICAGO MONEY MUSEUM

230 S. LaSalle Street, Chicago, IL 60604
(312) 322-2400
http://chicagofed.org/education/money-museum/index
Open 8:30 a.m.–5:00 p.m. Monday–Friday except on bank holidays.

Money, money, money! Who doesn't love it? Learn all about money and the Federal Reserve at the Money Museum. Before entry to the museum, you'll be required to participate in a security screening, and every adult is required to have a government-issued ID to enter. Once inside, you'll discover the history of trading and money, how money is designed and printed, and what the Federal Reserve does to help control the value of money. A short movie gives you some information about the Federal Reserve, and interactive displays let you put your own face on a bill, try your hand at controlling interest rates or deciding when to destroy damaged bills, or see what you look like standing next to a briefcase filled with one million dollars. Learn even more from the experts by taking a guided tour of the museum, offered at 1:00 p.m. daily (no reservation required).

FIELD MUSEUM OF NATURAL HISTORY

1400 S. Lake Shore Drive, Chicago, IL 60605
(312) 922-9410
www.fieldmuseum.org
Open 9:00 a.m.–5:00 p.m. every day except Christmas Day.

When you're REALLY famous, you only need one name—Madonna, Beyoncé, Prince, Adele, and, of course, SUE. On display at the Field Museum of Natural History, SUE is the largest, best-preserved, and most complete *T. rex* fossil ever found. At more than 40 feet long, SUE is sure to draw a gasp from new visitors. Learn about all the things SUE taught scientists about the *Tyrannosaurus rex,* and if you'd like to see SUE come alive, buy some tickets for the *Waking the* T. rex *3-D: The Story of SUE* movie.

That's definitely not all, though—the Field Museum has about 30 million specimens, although only about 1% of those are on display for the public; the rest are being stored or used for research. The permanent exhibits at the Field Museum tell a story about life on Earth, from the evolution of the planet to mummies of Ancient Egypt to the Pawnee Earth Lodge. Get a behind-the-scenes look at Field Museum staff at the Fossil Preparation Lab and the DNA Discovery Center. Highlights of the Field Museum include the dioramas of various habitats and animals, the Grainger Hall of Gems, and the Inside Ancient Egypt exhibit, where visitors can walk inside a tomb with 5,000-year-old hieroglyphs. Temporary exhibits are often on display as well.

The Crown Family PlayLab, geared toward kids from ages 2 to 6, is open Thursday through Monday from 10:00 a.m. to 4:00 p.m. Kids can bang on drums, dress like animals, discover fossils, and create projects.

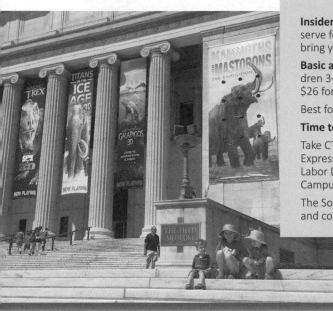

Insider tip: The Field Bistro and Museum Café serve food in the museum, but you can also bring your own.

Basic admission is $22 for adults, $15 for children 3–11. An All-Access Pass is $38 for adults, $26 for children 3–11.

Best for ages 5 and up.

Time to explore: 3–4 hours

Take CTA bus route #146 to Inner Drive/Michig Express/Museum Campus, or (mid-May throu Labor Day) take the #130 bus route to Museum Campus.

The Soldier Field Parking lot is near the museu and costs about $22.

HAROLD WASHINGTON LIBRARY
400 S. State Street, Chicago, IL 60605
(312) 747-4300
http://www.chipublib.org/locations/15/
9:00 a.m.–9:00 p.m. Monday–Friday, 9:00 a.m.–5:00 p.m. Saturday,
1:00 p.m.–5:00 p.m. Sunday

The Harold Washington Library, the central library of the Chicago Public Library system, opened in 1991 and was named for Chicago's first African-American mayor, who also spearheaded the effort to build the library before his death in 1987. The exterior is impressive, with giant arched windows and ornamental owls, but the real treasure lies inside. The central lobby, which has both a circulation desk and information desk, is two stories high and truly awe-inspiring. Younger kids will enjoy the enormous children's library on the second floor, where they can not only find their favorite books, but stage a puppet show, explore foreign language materials, or find inspiration for writing. Older kids will love the Maker Lab and the YOUmedia Center, a technology center for teens.

Explore all nine floors to see the original works from over 50 local and international artists, and make sure you visit the ninth-floor winter garden. Other perks: a variety of genealogy resources and Chicago's only free music practice rooms open to the public.

Tip: Check out the website before you plan your visit for a schedule of story times, book clubs, author events, art tours, and other events.

Free

Good for all ages.

Time to explore: 1–3 hours

Nearby parking garages charge about $15–$30.

Take the Brown, Pink, Orange, or Purple lines to Harold Washington Library—State/Van Buren subway station.

MAGGIE DALEY PARK

337 E. Randolph Street, Chicago, IL 60601
(312) 742-3918
http://www.chicagoparkdistrict.com/parks/maggie-daley-park/
Monday–Saturday 8:00 a.m.–10:00 p.m., Sunday 10:00 a.m.–10:00 p.m.

It may be a letdown to visit your local neighborhood park after a visit to the expansive and diverse Maggie Daley Park. With different zones for active and imaginative play for various age groups and abilities, this really is a park for every kid. The location between the skyscrapers and Lake Michigan make this one of the most scenic places in the city, especially with beautiful landscaping and art installations. Walk along the paths to different areas, including The Sea, The Harbor, and The Enchanted Forest.

The highlight of Maggie Daley Park is the Wave Lawn and Slide Crater. The colorful play structures contain plenty of nooks and crannies, talk tubes, slides, and a viewing scope. Parents can find a seat in the middle of it all on tiered wooden platforms.

If Chicago's too cold and icy for the playground, bring some ice skates for a glide around the quarter-mile ice skating ribbon. Rental skates are available for a fee if you don't have your own.

Insider tip: Maggie Daley is a very open park and it's often very busy, so it can be difficult to watch multiple children simultaneously. Bright colored clothing or accessories might make your kid(s) easier to spot in the crowd.

Free

Best for ages 12 and under.

Time to explore: 1–2 hours, maybe more!

Buses stop at upper Randolph and upper Columbus. The Red Line stops at State/Randall and State/Monroe about five blocks away. Green, Orange, Brown, Pink, and Purple lines stop at Randolph/Wabash or Madison/Wabash five blocks away.

Metered parking is available on upper Randolph Street. The Millennium Lakeside garage charges about $30.

MILLENNIUM PARK

201 E. Randolph Street, Chicago, IL 60602
(312) 742-1168
http://www.millenniumpark.org
Open 8:00 a.m.–11:00 p.m. daily

The history of Millennium Park is fascinating. Prior to the construction of the park, the land it now occupies was owned by the Illinois Central Railroad and was covered with railroad tracks. The construction of the park was fraught with controversy, and the cost swelled to more than three times the original budget, which was paid by both the city of Chicago and private donors. The opening was delayed four years to 2004, but even the strongest critics are pleased with the result. In fact, Millennium Park has been recognized with awards for accessibility, design, and environmental vision, and because public transportation and parking structures are below the park, it might just be one of the largest rooftop gardens in the world.

Millennium Park covers nearly 25 acres of lakefront land and welcomes millions of visitors every year. It's filled with open spaces, an abundance of sculptures and other works of art, and wheelchair-accessible features. Grab a meal at the Park Grill, bring a picnic lunch, or enjoy one of the many, many restaurants nearby.

These are features of Millennium Park you'll want to check out:

- Cloud Gate, or "the Bean" as many call it, is probably the most recognizable attraction in Millennium Park. The giant stainless steel sculpture reflects the skyline of the city, and its concave interior generates fascinating reflections for those who step under it.

- Crown Fountain is another spectacular work of art composed of two 50-foot glass towers facing each other with a wading pool between them. Each tower displays faces of Chicagoans, and sometimes they "spit" water from their mouth—great for getting wet on hot summer days.

- The Lurie Garden is a 2.5-acre four-season garden edged with 15-foot-tall hedges. Free tours of the garden are offered on Thursdays, Fridays, and Sundays.

- The Pritzker Pavilion hosts a variety of music performances—everything from classical to house music to Mariachi. There are 4,000 seats in the pavilion and lawn seating for an additional 7,000 people.

- The BP Bridge is a winding path bordered by brushed steel panels that takes pedestrians over Columbus Drive. It's functional, accessible, and absolutely beautiful.

- The Nichols Bridgeway is a pedestrian walkway over Monroe that runs from the Great Lawn of Millennium Park to the third floor of the Art Institute. Kids will love running up and down the bridgeway, and it's a great place to enjoy the view and take pictures.

Insider tip: If you want to see the whole park and learn more, there are free tours of Millennium Park at 11:30 a.m. and 1:00 p.m. daily from late May until early October. These are offered on a "first-come, first-served" basis.

Free

Good for all ages.

Time to explore: Anywhere from 1 hour to all day.

The Metra Electric and South Shore lines stop at Millennium Park Station under Millennium Park. Green, Orange, Brown, Pink, and Purple lines stop at Madison/Wabash and Randolph/Wabash two blocks away; Red and Blue lines stop at Monroe or Washington, about three blocks away. Multiple CTA buses stop nearby.

Millennium Park, Grant Park North, Grant Park South, and East Monroe parking garages are all available nearby, with rates about $30–$35. Early bird rate is $16.

MUSEUM OF CONTEMPORARY ART

220 East Chicago Avenue, Chicago, IL 60611
(312) 280-2660
http://www2.mcachicago.org/
Tuesday 10:00 a.m.–8:00 p.m., Wednesday–Sunday 10:00 a.m.–5:00 p.m.

Although smaller than most of the other major Chicago museums, the Museum of Contemporary Art is constantly changing and offering new experiences to visitors. Temporary exhibits sometimes include art pieces on the sidewalk in front of the building. The MCA Café offers lunch and dinner with plenty of options kids will like, including bagels, yogurt parfaits, and burgers, and the lowest level of the museum has a theatre for performances and presentations. Stop at the gift shop for souvenirs or a unique gift, and if the weather allows, be sure to take a walk in the sculpture garden outside.

The MCA has free family days about once a month (see their website for specific dates), with activities, art projects, and entertainment. The MCA even offers stroller tours on the first Wednesday of each month so parents of babies can enjoy the exhibits without anxiety about them fussing or crying.

As with any art museum, it may be best to research the current exhibits before visiting, as some are adult-themed.

Insider tip: To avoid the crowds, visit on Wednesday or Thursday. If you can handle a crowd, Tuesdays are free Illinois resident admission days, and SOAR market is also outdoors on Tuesdays from June to October.

Suggested donation is $12 for adults, $7 for students. Children under 12 get in free. Illinois residents receive free admission on Tuesdays.

Good for all ages.

Time to explore: 1–3 hours

MCA Parking Garage costs about $30–$40.

Four blocks east of Red Line at Chicago Avenue; #10 Museum or #66 Chicago Avenue buses.

NAVY PIER

600 E. Grand Avenue, Chicago, IL 60611
(312) 595-7437
https://navypier.com/
Saturday 10:00 a.m.–10:00 p.m., Sunday 10:00 a.m.–7:00 p.m., Monday–Thursday 10:00 a.m.–8:00 p.m., Friday 10:00 a.m.–10:00 p.m.

Navy Pier is one of the most popular tourist attractions in Chicago for good reason—it's in the center of the city, with beautiful views of the lakefront and the skyline and has attractions that will appeal to every member of the family. Many Chicago natives dismiss it as being "too touristy," but attractions like the Chicago Children's Museum, the Chicago Shakespeare Theater, Amazing Chicago's Funhouse Maze, and the Ferris Wheel make it a great destination for all families—visitors and locals. There's plenty of shopping and restaurants, but expect some crowds. Navy Pier is also the launching point for a variety of boat tours and specialty cruises.

Navy Pier hosts special events and festivals at different times of the year, including the Chicago Flower and Garden Show in the spring, free summer fireworks, Tall Ships Chicago in the summer, a Halloween celebration in October, and Winter Wonderfest in December and January.

It is easy to spend a lot of money at Navy Pier, but it's not necessary. Frugal families can walk and play along the lakeshore, browse the free Driehaus Gallery of Stained Glass, and the bring a picnic lunch to enjoy in the Crystal Gardens—a one-acre, six-story-high atrium with fountains, palm trees, and seasonal flowers.

Insider tip: The food court can be very crowded, especially on weekends. Instead, pack a lunch and enjoy a picnic outside or in the Crystal Gardens.

FREE—There is no admission to Navy Pier, but there are fees for many of the attractions.

Good for all ages.

Time to explore: 3 hours to all day

Multiple CTA buses stop at Navy Pier, as well as water taxis, sightseeing buses, and trolleys.

Two parking garages; parking costs about $30.

OPEN BOOKS CHICAGO
651 W. Lake Street, Chicago, IL 60661
(312) 475-1355
http://www.open-books.org/
9:00 a.m.–7:00 p.m. Monday–Saturday, noon–6:00 p.m. Sunday

Ernest Hemingway said, "There is no friend as loyal as a book," and if he's right, then there are 50,000 best friends waiting for you here. Open is what all readers dream of—a loft with brick walls filled with over 50,000 books. There's a dedicated youth section where kids can hunker down in a comfy chair and flip through one of the more than 10,000 kids' books available here. Check their schedule for special story times and book signings, and you can inquire about rental space for a child's birthday party.

Open Books is more than an amazing bookstore—it's a community move-ment. This non-profit organization accepts donations of used books that are then sold in their flagship store on Lake Street and at their additional location in the Pilsen neighborhood of Chicago. Open Books donates books through book grants to students and educators, and they offer instructional programs for kids from second through twelfth grade, including Reading Buddies, creative writing workshops, ReadthenWrite, and Publishing Academy.

Insider tip: Can't find exactly what you're looking for? Leave your information and Open Books will contact you when the book you request is donated.

Free to browse.

Good for all ages.

Time to explore: 1–2 hours

Three blocks from the Ogilvie Metra stop. Two blocks from Clinton stop for the Green and Pink lines, and the #8 and #16 bus routes.

Pay lots are available nearby.

PEDWAY

http://www.cityofchicago.org/city/en/depts/cdot/provdrs/ped/srvs/pedway.html
Open 7:00 a.m.–5:00 p.m. Monday through Friday.

While thousands of people navigate the sidewalks of Chicago, there is an entire system of interconnected tunnels that also run beneath the streets. The Chicago Pedway covers five miles and connects more than 50 buildings and attractions including Millennium Park, the Palmer House Hilton, the Harold Washington Library, Swissotel, Aon Center, the Chicago Board of Trade, Macy's, and the Daley Center. Entry points are marked by yellow star signs you may have passed many times without even noticing.

Besides providing weather protection to commuters and visitors, the Pedway also has stores and restaurants, including many with sandwiches and other on-the-go selections.

Tip: The Pedway is not always clearly marked and can be confusing. Consider a tour or stick to major areas.

Free

Good for all ages.

Time to explore: Varies depending on your purpose and destination.

Transportation and parking vary depending on the entry and exit points. The Pedway connects to more than 50 buildings and can be used to walk from one destination to another.

PINSTRIPES

435 E. Illinois Street, Chicago, IL 60611
(312) 527-3010
www.pinstripes.com/chicago-illinois
Open 11:30 a.m.–11:00 p.m. Monday through Thursday, 11:30 a.m.–1:00 a.m.
Friday, 10:00 a.m.–1:00 a.m. Saturday, and 10:00 a.m.–10:00 p.m. Sunday.

If you think of molded plastic seats, harsh lighting, and soggy nachos when
someone mentions heading to a bowling alley, you will be very pleasantly surprised by a trip to Pinstripes. Yes, there's still bowling, but nothing else about it
will seem familiar. Pinstripes is sophisticated and plush, with lots of comfortable
seating, a full restaurant with bistro cuisine, and an outdoor patio with fire pits.
Pinstripes also offers indoor bocce ball.

Forget the soggy nachos, because the bistro serves calamari, flatbread, and
house-made gelato. Kids' meals include a starter, entree, beverage, and dessert
for $9.

Private events—everything from a child's birthday party to a class field trip to
weddings—are a Pinstripes specialty. They also have special events, including
things like brunch with Santa and pumpkin carving. Bumper bowling is available,
and if you visit on weekdays from 10:00 a.m. to noon for Kids Bowling Club, kids
bowl for only $3 per hour with $3 shoe rental, and parents bowl free.

Insider tip: Ask about wristbands. If you get your hands on one, you'll be able to
use it to get your choice of a free glass of wine, root beer float, or ice cream
sundae every time you visit.

$8–$16/hour for bowling, $5 for shoes rental (comes with a free pair of Pinstripes
socks for you to keep), $5–$12/hour for bocce.

Best for ages 3 and up.

Time to explore: 3–4 hours

CTA bus routes #2, #29, #65, #66, and #124 stop at Illinois and Peshtigo.

Valet parking is available for $16.

JOHN G. SHEDD AQUARIUM

1200 S. Lake Shore Drive, Chicago, IL 60605
(312) 939-2438
http://www.sheddaquarium.org
Open 9:00 a.m.–6:00 p.m. weekends, 9:00 a.m.–5:00 p.m. weekdays. Open 9:00
a.m.–6:00 p.m. daily during the summer (mid-June to late August).

There's something relaxing and magical about watching fish gliding through
the water, and you can see them up close at the Shedd Aquarium. Visit the Ama-
zon, the Caribbean, the Wild Reef, and the Waters of the World to see a wide
range of aquatic habitats and animals. The Aquatic Presentation lets you see and
hear sea lions, beluga whales, and dolphins and see how they interact with their

trainers. Stingray Touch, which allows you to get up close to a pool of stingrays, is open late May through October.

Kids will especially love the Polar Play Zone, where they can pretend to be a penguin or a deep-sea explorer, and the 4-D experience, where enhancements like misting water and bubbles are added to a 3-D movie.

The Shedd Aquarium is the most-visited cultural attraction in Chicago, with about two million visitors per year. Unfortunately, that means it can get busy. Expect a long line to get in, sometimes as long as 2 hours, so arrive early and dress for the weather, because you'll likely be waiting outside.

Insider tip: The Shedd Aquarium offers free days for Illinois residents and these days are VERY popular. If you do not need to take advantage of the free admission (for instance, if you are not from Illinois or if you have a membership), it's a good idea to check out when these dates occur and avoid them.

General admission is $8 for adults, $6 for children ages 3–11; children under 3 are free. Passes that include all exhibits, shows, and additional experiences start at about $22 for children and $31 for adults. Priority entry and express passes are also available for an additional fee.

Good for all ages.

Time to explore: 3–4 hours.

CTA bus #146 stops at the Museum Campus, where the aquarium is located. (Please note: #146 to Harrison/State will NOT take you all the way to the museum, so make sure it says "Museum Campus.")

There is a very limited amount of metered parking on the street. Parking in lots and garages near the Shedd will cost about $11–$22 and may be limited or more expensive when there is a game or event at Soldier Field.

SKYDECK CHICAGO AT THE WILLIS (FORMERLY SEARS) TOWER

233 S. Wacker Drive, Chicago, IL 60606
(312) 875-9447
www.theskydeck.com
Open 365 days a year; 10:00 a.m.–8:00 p.m. from October through February,
and 9:00 a.m.–10:00 p.m. from March through September.

Although the Willis Tower is no longer the tallest building in the world (it held
that record from 1973 to 1998), it still has the highest observation deck in the
United States. The Skydeck is on the 103rd floor of the Willis Tower, and you can
see some astounding things from 1,353 feet up; in fact, on a clear day, visitors
can see up to four states—Illinois, Indiana, Wisconsin, and Michigan.

Of course, once you're up there you need the entire experience, which means
stepping out onto the Ledge. A 4.3-foot glass cube protrudes from the side of
the Skydeck allowing you to have a full, unobstructed view of the city, even
under your feet! Fear not—the ledge is made from three layers of half-inch-
thick glass and has a capacity of 10,000 pounds—no amount of shaking or even
jumping will put you in danger. Photos are a must, and professional photos are
available from Skydeck staff if you want to ensure a good shot.

There's sometimes confusion over the name of the building; locals will tell you
that "Willis" is pronounced "Sears," the building's former name, but now you
know they're one and the same.

Family bathrooms are located on the lower level, and you can bring strollers
up to the Skydeck. The best time to visit to avoid crowds is right at opening or
after 5:00 p.m.

Insider tip: Lines can be long, and even Fast Pass holders may not be able to
avoid all the lines. There are some interactive displays and activities, but bring
something to keep the kids occupied while you wait.

Admission is $22 for adults, $14 for children ages 3–11. Children under 3 are free.
Fast Pass admission is available for $49 per person.

Good for all ages.

Time to explore: 1–2 hours

Multiple CTA buses stop within a block of the building on Adams, Wacker, and
Jackson. The Brown, Orange, Purple, and Pink lines stop at Quincy/Wells.

Parking is available at InterPark at 211 W. Adams, and it will be about $35.

SOD ROOM

1454 South Michigan Avenue, 2nd floor, Chicago, IL 60605
(312) 922-3131
http://www.sodroom.com
Open for drop-in play 9:30 a.m.–5:30 p.m. Monday–Friday; weekend hours vary depending on private party schedules.

Sod Room has a simple, uncluttered feel, with high ceilings, exposed brick walls, and lots of natural light. The owners—Chicago parents—pride themselves on creating an eco-friendly play space that encourages parents to find other members of the natural lifestyle community. From the recycled cork floor, to the low VOC paint, to the reclaimed wood, green is the theme at Sod Room, but all kids will notice is the swing, the colorful cork wall, and the selection of toys (all safe, sustainable, and responsibly made).

If you're looking for more than open play, Sod Room has workshops and classes, and they host private parties. The small retail boutique carries local, organic, and fair trade toys and gifts.

While parents supervise their kids, they can enjoy complimentary coffee or tea and free wifi. Just don't forget your socks! Every visitor must wear socks, even adults.

Tip: Bring your own snacks or food; outside food is allowed in the designated area.

$12 per child; siblings are $8. Babies 0–6 months are free with a paid sibling or $6 without a sibling. Memberships and multi-visit passes are available.

Best for children 5 and under.

Time to explore: 1–2 hours

Roosevelt Street station and several CTA buses are within a few blocks.

Metered parking is available on Michigan Avenue.

TRIBUNE TOWER

435 N. Michigan Avenue, Chicago, IL 60611
http://www.chicagoarchitecture.org/2013/03/05/pictures-of-all-149-rocks-stuck-on-the-tribune-tower/ (This is an unofficial site that includes photos of all landmarks incorporated into the building's facade.)
Best to visit during daylight hours.

Who knew you could see pieces of the White House, the Aztec ruins, and the Sydney Opera House right here in Chicago? The Tribune Tower is home to—you guessed it—the legendary Chicago Tribune, and the stone walls in the lobby are inscribed with quotes about freedom of speech and freedom of the press. The really cool stuff, however, is outside. The facade of the Tribune Tower is embedded with pieces of famous and historical locations from all around the world. There are nearly 150 fragments from notable places, including the Cathedral of Notre Dame, the Taj Mahal, the Alamo, the former World Trade Center, the Great Wall of China, and Abraham Lincoln's tomb. See how many you can spot! Also, WGN Radio windows are on the ground floor, so you can take a peek at local radio personalities and guests.

Tip: This is an outdoor activity, so dress for the weather. This is also a great photo opportunity! Show friends how you visited (a piece of) several historical sites within a matter of minutes!

Free

Best for ages 5 and up.

Time to explore: 1 hour or less

Parking garages are nearby; you're unlikely to find street parking.

There are bus stops nearby—Michigan and Hubbard and Illinois (lower) and St. Clair.

URBAN ADVENTURE QUEST

The Loop
(866) 863-4577
http://www.urbanquest.com/purchaseaquest?city=Chicago
Recommended during daylight hours

Dorothy had Oz, Frodo had Middle Earth, and your mission (should you choose to accept it) is to journey through Chicago.

With the use of clues and optional hints on your smart phone, Urban Adventure Quest will lead you on an interactive tour from the Westin Chicago River North to Monroe and Dearborn. In between you'll see highlights like the riverfront, Hard Rock Hotel, The Bean, the Art Institute, and the Palmer House. There are no set times or dates, so start your quest when it's convenient and wear comfortable shoes because you'll cover two or three miles. The quest takes about two hours to complete, and although there are no prizes, you will get bragging rights, see famous sites and hidden gems, and learn interesting facts along the way.

Insider tip: Charge your phone before starting your quest, and consider bringing a back-up charger.

$49 for a team of 2–5 people.

Recommended for children and adults of any age who are able to walk two to three miles.

WATER TOWER PLACE

835 N. Michigan Avenue, Chicago, IL 60611
(312) 440-3166
http://shopwatertower.com
Open 10:00 a.m.–9:00 p.m. Monday–Saturday, 11:00 a.m.–6:00 p.m. Sunday.
Individual stores and restaurants may have hours that vary from mall hours.

Its location on the Magnificent Mile puts Water Tower Place right at the heart of the city, and unusual features like the fountain alongside the escalators at the main entrance and glass elevator make it an interesting place to explore, with or without spending any money. If you are in the mood to shop, it's definitely the place to be, with eight levels and over 100 shops. Shops include favorites like the LEGO Store and Build-A-Bear, as well as some unique places like Candyality and the American Girl flagship store. In addition to shopping, you can check out The Art of Dr. Seuss Gallery and Harry Carey's Sports Museum. The food court on the lower level offers a variety of fresh food options, and there are shops offering snacks, treats, and fast food throughout the mall.

Sports

CHICAGO BEARS

Soldier Field, 1410 Museum Campus Drive, Chicago, IL 60605
(312) 235-7000
http://www.chicagobears.com/
Season runs September through January.

There are few people more revered in Chicago than "Da Coach" Mike Ditka. He's no longer the coach of "Da Bears," but Chicagoans take football seriously, and they'll never forget the 1985 Super Bowl win. Aside from the football game, the coach and players became stars and performed the Super Bowl Shuffle (which was filmed before the playoffs!). Football legends Dick Butkus, Walter Payton, Jim McMahon, William "the Refrigerator" Perry, and Brian Urlacher have all been part of the Bears team.

Bundle up because it gets cold during football season, and be sure to get there extra early for hours of tailgating. One of the biggest rivalries in the NFL is between the Chicago Bears and the Green Bay Packers, so try to avoid the Packers colors (green/yellow) when you visit, or be prepared for some backlash from the devoted Bears fans. Tickets sell out fast, so buy them ASAP.

Insider tip: If you can't swing the $100+ tickets, plan for a trip to the Family Fest they hold in early August before the season starts. Tickets start at about $10 and there are plenty of kid-friendly activities to enjoy.

Tickets start at about $115.

Games usually last about 3 hours.

The stadium is a few blocks east of the Roosevelt stops on the CTA Red, Orange and Green lines. CTA bus #128 Soldier Field Express or the #130 Museum Campus will also take you to Soldier Field.

There are several lots and garages near Soldier Field, and prices range from $25 to $106 for parking. Some lots only accept cash, so your best bet is to purchase parking online before you go.

Food

BUBBA GUMP SHRIMP CO.
Navy Pier, 700 E. Grand Avenue, #131, Chicago, IL 60611
(312) 252-4867
www.bubbagump.com/locations/chicago
Open for lunch and dinner daily

Like Bubba told Forrest Gump, you can do just about anything with shrimp: "You can barbecue it, boil it, broil it, bake it, sauté it. There's shrimp-kabobs, shrimp creole, shrimp gumbo. Pan fried, deep fried, stir-fried. There's pineapple shrimp, lemon shrimp, coconut shrimp, pepper shrimp, shrimp soup, shrimp stew, shrimp salad, shrimp and potatoes, shrimp burger, shrimp sandwich. That, that's about it." And yes, just about all of that is on the menu at Bubba Gump Shrimp Co., but that's not all. There's also a wide variety of seafood besides shrimp, salads, chicken, ribs, and steak.

Although Navy Pier isn't exactly seaside, the southern seashore decor will make you feel like it is. There's also plenty of Forrest Gump memorabilia and a souvenir gift shop. Outdoor seating is available seasonally, and kids will love the large selection of entrees and sides on the kids' menu. Kids' meals come with a fountain beverage and Jell-O dessert, but you can also upgrade to a Slushie and a Build Your Own Sundae.

Kids' meals are about $8. Most entrees are $20–$30.

Multiple CTA buses stop at Navy Pier, as well as water taxis, sightseeing buses, and trolleys.

Two parking garages; parking costs about $30.

DYLAN'S CANDY BAR
445 N. Michigan Avenue, Chicago, IL 60611
(312) 702-2247
https://www.dylanscandybar.com/info/chicago.html
10:00 a.m.–9:00 p.m. Monday–Thursday, 10:00 a.m.–10:00 p.m. Friday and Saturday, 11:00 a.m.–8:00 p.m. Sunday

From the moment you set foot in Dylan's Candy Bar, the large, bright, bold decorations provide a bit of eye candy that's sure to get your mouth watering, including an array of giant lollipops reaching all the way up to the second story. Yes, that's two stories of candy.

Can you say epic sugar coma? Dylan's Candy Bar can get you there. Dylan's has every kind of candy you can imagine, both in bulk and prewrapped, plus a fudge bar and a counter where you can buy personalized candy. It's a little overwhelming, but definitely a fun splurge that adults and children are sure to remember forever. Dylan's also has lots of non-food "candy" items like t-shirts, bags, and pajamas.

Need something to wash down all that candy? Dylan's Candy Bar Café has cocktails and mocktails, as well as a full menu of both sweet and savory items for lunch or dinner.

Insider tip: Dylan's is located in the Tribune Tower. As you're munching on your sugary treats, you can walk around the building to find 149 different stone fragments from landmarks all over the world.

Free to browse

All ages

1 hour or less

Parking garages are nearby; you're unlikely to find street parking.

There are bus stops nearby—Michigan and Hubbard and Illinois (lower) and St. Clair.

FOGO DE CHÃO BRAZILIAN STEAKHOUSE

661 N. LaSalle Street, Chicago, IL 60654
(312) 932-9330
http://www.fogodechao.com
Open for lunch and dinner daily

If you haven't experienced a Brazilian steakhouse, you're missing out, and it's time to change that. Fogo de Chão offers a variety of meat prepared in the churrasco Brazilian grilling style and serves it from giant skewers brought table to table by gauchos.

Although it's an upscale restaurant, the full churrasco experience makes it perfect for families. Visit the Market Table to choose from seasonal salads, fresh veggies, imported meats, cheeses, and artisan bread. Then, relax and allow the food to come to you—mashed potatoes and polenta first, and then meat at your own pace. The huge variety and all-you-can-eat style make this perfect for kids, whether they are adventurous eaters looking for new things to try, or picky eaters who will try one bite and not like something; even the picky eaters will find something they enjoy.

There's no set dress code, but business casual is a good bet. Reservations aren't required, but they are encouraged.

Lunch or dinner for each adult is about $35–$55 for the full churrasco experience; children ages 7–12 are half price, and kids 6 and under are free.

Take CTA bus route #156 to the LaSalle and Huron stop across from Fogo de Chão, or the CTA #22 route to Clark and Huron, about a block away.

Valet parking will cost $10–$13.

GINO'S EAST

162 E. Superior Street, Chicago, IL 60611
(312) 266-3337
http://www.ginoseast.com/locations/superior#home
Open for lunch and dinner daily

Chicago and deep dish pizza go together like peanut butter and jelly (although the former is much tastier!) and Gino's East is one of the most beloved places to grab a slice. Gino's has been serving deep dish pizza for 50 years and has expanded to several locations throughout the city of Chicago and the suburbs, as well as a few in Texas and Arizona. The location on Superior is the original, and they serve thick, crumbly crust with a bit of corn flavor; chunky, tangy sauce with lots of oregano; and cheese. Tons and tons of cheese. Meat-eaters can choose from crumbled or patty sausage. Although they didn't always, Gino's East does serve thin crust pizza, but why would you want that when you can have deep dish? Along the same lines, they have sandwiches, salads, and other non-pizza menu items.

Bring markers or a white correction pen when you go. You can write on the walls, tables, or pretty much anywhere. Gino's East has made itself a shrine for the graffiti of all its past pizza patrons.

Entrees are about $10–$15. A build-your-own deep dish pizza starts at $24.

Multiple CTA buses make stops along Michigan Avenue and Chicago Avenue. The CTA Red Line trains stop at the Chicago station about half a mile away.

Valet parking is $15 for 3 hours. Street parking is nearly impossible; there are parking garages nearby, but you'll pay about $30.

SOUTH WATER KITCHEN

Hotel Monaco Chicago, 225 N. Wabash Avenue, Chicago, IL 60601
(312) 236-9300
www.southwaterkitchen.com
Open for breakfast, lunch, and dinner daily

Looking for some sophisticated comfort food? South Water Kitchen is your destination. Located within the Hotel Monaco, South Water Kitchen specializes in Midwestern fare, with a focus on local and seasonal ingredients. With brick walls and dark wood, the atmosphere is elegant, warm, and comfortable. Adults can have a grown-up meal of risotto, lamb shoulder, or duck breast, while kids have options like macaroni and cheese, grilled chicken breast, or mini cheeseburgers. South Water Kitchen also has a huge gluten-free menu, cocktails, and decadent desserts like buttermilk beignets with vanilla bean ice cream and powdered sugar.

Kids' meals are about $10; entrees are in the $15–$30 range.

Brown, Orange, Purple, Green, and Pink lines stop at State/Lake just a couple blocks away.

Street parking is rare; there are multiple parking garages in the area with prices ranging from about $25 to $50.

Free Activities

- **Millennium Park**—Check out your reflection(s) in Cloud Gate and splash around in the Crown Fountain. Stroll the Lurie Garden, picnic on the lawn of the Pritzker Pavilion, and get a great view of the city from the Nichols Bridgeway.

- **Tour Millennium Park or the Lurie Garden**—Take a free tour of Millennium Park or the Lurie Garden. No registration is required. See the City of Chicago: Millennium Park website for days, times, and more details.

- **Pedway**—Get down. Literally. Travel the underground Pedway, which covers five miles and connects 50 buildings.

- **Federal Reserve Bank of Chicago Museum**—Find out what a million dollars looks like and take home a special souvenir. This is the only free activity in Chicago where you'll actually leave with more money than you came with (but it will be shredded!).

- **City Gallery at the Historic Water Tower**—Step inside the Historic Water Tower to check out the current exhibit.

- **Museum of Contemporary Photography**—Bored with Instagrammed photos of food? See something a little different.

- **Navy Pier**—Sure, it's touristy, but it is a nice place to walk along the water and see some free fireworks in the summer.

- **Buckingham Fountain**—This is a fun stop in the evening with the music and light display happening every 20 minutes beginning at dusk.

- **Chicago Architecture Foundation**—See the city from above—kinda. The Chicago Architecture Foundation has the largest, most complete replica of the downtown Loop area in the world.

- **The Chicago Cultural Center**—The Chicago Cultural Center offers visitor information, free tours, and a variety of free music, dance, theater, and family events.

- **Story Corps**—Everyone has a story to tell. Play the interviewer (or interviewee) and record it at the Chicago Cultural Center to be archived and possibly aired on WBEZ 91.5 FM.

- **Tribune Tower**—Stones from 120 famous landmarks are embedded in the Tribune Tower. Can you find them all?

- **Puppet Bike**—This stage on wheels travels the streets of Chicago and stops to do free shows for anyone lucky enough to happen upon it.

- **Maggie Daley Park**—It's brand new and not to be missed. Not only are there epic bridges, slides, and play structures, but there's plenty of green space and gardens to enjoy too.

- **Family Fun Fest**—From late June to late August, Millennium Park is the spot for the Family Fun Fest, a free festival from 10:00 a.m. to 2:00 p.m. every day, with performances, activities, and art projects.

NORTH SIDE (INCLUDING FAR NORTH AND NORTHWEST)

As you head north in Chicago, the buildings grow smaller and the green space grows larger. The North Side is not as busy as downtown, but it's a popular place for young families. There's still plenty to do, great places to dine, and lots of fun activities for families. Parking can still be limited in some places, especially near Wrigley Field and other popular attractions, but public transportation is plentiful.

Attractions

BLUE MAN GROUP
The Briar Street Theater, 3133 N. Halsted Street, Chicago, IL 60657
(773) 739-2463
www.BlueMan.com/Chicago
Show times vary.

Blue Man Group has been performing in Chicago since 1997, so there's a good chance that if you've lived here a while you've already seen it. If you haven't, you're really missing something, and if you have—you need to go again and bring the kids. With a cast of bizarre, non-speaking blue characters, and a rock concert/dance party feel, Blue Man Group provides a comedic show that feels like it's also a collaborative art project. The combination of music, technology, and comedy is difficult to describe and impossible to forget, and it'll definitely get you dancing at your seat.

Blue Man Group has partnered with local hotels, attractions, and restaurants to offer packages and discounts, so check out their current specials on the website. They also offer special autism-friendly performances that are slightly modified to reduce the sound and they strive to create a calming environment in the lobby for audience members who may need a break from the show.

Insider tip: Noise-reducing headphones are available (and strongly encouraged) for young or sensitive children.

Tickets are approximately $50–$100 each.

For ages 3 and up only; children under the age of 3 are not permitted.

Time to explore: 2–3 hours

Parking is $15, cash only.

The #8 Halsted bus, #22 Clark bus, #77 Belmont bus, and #156 LaSalle bus stop near the Briar Street Theater.

EMERALD CITY THEATRE

2936 N. Southport Avenue, Chicago, IL 60657
(773) 529-2690
www.emeraldcitytheatre.com
Show dates and times vary; most shows are between 10:00 a.m. and 1:00 p.m.

Shows at:

- Apollo Theatre, 2540 N. Lincoln Avenue, Chicago, IL 60614

- Little Theatre, 2933 N. Southport Avenue, Chicago, IL 60657

- Broadway Playhouse, 175 E. Chestnut, Chicago, IL 60611 (north side of Water Tower Place)

There's no such thing as being too young for stage productions, especially thanks to organizations like the Emerald City Theatre. Emerald City Theatre is a non-profit organization—reaching about 80,000 people annually—that seeks to inspire early learners with play. A variety of family-friendly shows are offered each season, and classes and camps are offered for children as young as three years old. Study guides are provided for each show to help parents and teachers reinforce show themes through further discussion and activities. Emerald City Theatre welcomes schools and organizations to attend shows, and grants are available for school programs. Shows are approximately 1 hour long with no intermission.

Insider tip: Plan to arrive early and stay late—there's always a pre-show activity in the lobby related to the show, and characters from the show will be available in the lobby after performances for questions, photos, and autographs.

Tickets are generally about $18–$30.

Age recommendations vary according to the shows. Plays at the Little Theatre are generally appropriate for ages 0–5. Other performances may be appropriate for children as young as 3 or as old as 12, depending on the show.

Time to explore: About 2 hours

Apollo Theatre—Take Red, Brown, or Purple Line to Fullerton Stop. Valet parking available for $10; free and metered parking on streets.

Little Theatre—Take the Brown Line train to the Wellington stop or the CTA bus route #9 to Ashland Street and Wellington Avenue or the route #11 to Lincoln and Wellington. Street parking is available.

Broadway Playhouse—Take the Red Line train to Chicago and walk five blocks, or the Brown or Purple Line train to Chicago and walk 10 blocks to the theater. Parking in garage for $11–$14.

BUILDING BLOCKS TOY STORE

3306 N. Lincoln Avenue, Chicago, IL 60657
(773) 525-6200
2130 W. Division Street, Chicago, IL 60622
(773) 235-1888
www.BuildingBlocksToys.com
Monday–Friday 10:00 a.m.–7:00 p.m., Saturday 9:30 a.m.–6:00 p.m., Sunday
9:30 a.m.–5:00 p.m.

Building Blocks Toy Store is the product of self-described "play ambassador" Katherine McHenry. Both locations carry a wide variety of educational and developmental toys in a range of prices, from brands like Melissa and Doug, Alex, Educational Insights, Hape, and Green Toys, and if the stock is overwhelming, the employees are happy to make recommendations so you can find just the right toy. There's a play area in each store so kids can test out some toys or stay busy playing while you shop. Building Blocks is committed to the community. They often host special events and promotions and contribute to local organizations. You'll find extra perks here you won't find at most stores, like a generous return policy and free delivery within two miles of the store.

Insider tip: Do all your gift shopping here. Not only is the staff great at making recommendations, but gifts are wrapped for free.

Free to browse and play.

Good for all ages.

Time to explore: 1–2 hours

Lincoln Park—CTA bus route #11 stops at Lincoln and School/Marshfield. Brown Line train stops at Paulina, a block away.

Division—CTA bus route #70 stops at Division and Hoyne. Half a mile to Blue Line train stop at Division and Damen.

Street parking is available.

CHICAGO HISTORY MUSEUM

1601 N. Clark Street, Chicago, IL 60614
(312) 642-4600
www.chicagohs.org
Open 9:30 a.m.–4:30 p.m. Monday through Saturday, noon–5:00 p.m. Sunday

Just the word "history" sometimes elicits groans from children, but the Chicago History Museum will delight even the most skeptical kid, with bright displays, plenty of interactive exhibits, and fascinating facts. Climb aboard an old "L" car, check out vintage fashions and games from decades past, and watch a short film about some of the major events in Chicago's history while you're there. The youngest visitors will especially love the Sensing Chicago exhibit, where they can feel what it's like to ride a high wheel bike on old-fashioned streets, smell Chicago's past (chocolate factory anyone?), and be part of a traditional Chicago hot dog.

Right now, you can also learn about the Secret Lives of Objects, including things like Ann Landers's electric typewriter, Charlie Chaplin's cane, and eyeglasses belonging to Nathan Leopold Jr. of the Leopold and Loeb trial. This exhibit will only be around until 2018, but it's definitely worth checking out.

The Chicago History Museum has a museum store and the North & Clark Café, which serves sandwiches, soups, salads, and all-day breakfast.

Insider tip: For a great free souvenir, the Sensing Chicago exhibit lets you create a Chicago postcard with your photo and email it.

Admission is $16 per adult; children 12 and under are free. Admission is free on Tuesdays from 12:30 p.m. to 7:30 p.m. for Illinois residents.

Best for ages 3 and up.

Time to explore: 3–4 hours

CTA buses #22, #36, #72, #73, #151, and #156 stop near the museum; half a mile from the Brown Line stop at Sedgwick and the Red Line stop at Clark/Division.

$9 parking in the lot with validation.

EXPLORE & MUCH MORE
3827 N. Southport Avenue, Chicago, IL 60613
(773) 880-5437
www.exploreandmuchmore.com
Open 9:00 a.m.–5:00 p.m. Monday through Friday. Weekend hours vary.

Brighten up a dreary Chicago day with a visit to the bright and colorful Explore & Much More indoor play area. There are two floors of entertainment here, including slides, a bounce house, play structures, a light table, shopping area, reading nook, and much more. Besides open play, Explore & Much More is a great place for parties or special events. Coffee is free on weekdays, but bring your own food; there is a separate area where visitors can eat. All visitors must wear socks; socks can be purchased for $2 a pair.

Insider tip: Check the online schedule to see when classes are offered. Explore & Much More offers classes every weekday in Music and Movement or Arts and Crafts, and they are included in the price of admission.

Admission for the whole day is $12 for the first child, $9 for a sibling. Adults and non-crawlers are free.

Best for children 6 months through 8 years old.

Time to explore: 2–3 hours

CTA bus route #22 stops at Clark and Byron, routes #9 and #80 stop at Irving Park and Southport; both are a couple blocks away.

Metered street parking is available.

FOSTER BEACH

5200 N. Lake Shore Drive, Chicago, IL 60640
(312) 742-5121
http://www.cpdbeaches.com/beaches/foster-beach/
11:00 a.m.–7:00 p.m. daily.

The beach is probably not the first thing that pops into your mind when you think of the city of Chicago, but Chicago does have some impressive beaches along the many miles of Lake Michigan shore. Montrose, North Avenue, and Oak Street are popular beaches you're likely to hear about, but for families Foster Beach is an excellent choice. A little farther north of downtown, Foster Beach has cheap or free parking that you won't find at some of the other beaches. It's large, clean, and has amenities like lifeguards, a beach house with concessions and bathrooms, and even bike rentals are available. All of this has earned Foster Beach a reputation as a good family beach, so you're likely to find lots of parents and kids there. If the sun gets to be too much, there's shade in the attached park.

Insider tip: Check before going, because there are occasional swim advisories due to fluctuations in water quality.

Free

Good for all ages.

Time to explore: 1 hour to all day

CTA Red Line (Berwyn) half a mile west. CTA buses #147, #136, #146 at Foster and Marine Drive a couple blocks away.

Pay and display lot.

GOLDFISH SWIM SCHOOL

2630 W. Bradley Place, Chicago, IL 60618
(773) 588-7946
www.roscoevillage.goldfishswimschool.com
Open 9:00 a.m.–8:00 p.m. Monday, Thursday, and Friday; 9:00 a.m.–7:30 p.m.
Tuesday and Wednesday; 8:30 a.m.–8:00 p.m. Saturday; 9:00 a.m.–6:00 p.m.
Sunday.

There are times when it's hard to imagine any part of Chicago being warm, but
no matter how frigid the outdoor weather is, the pool at Goldfish Swim School
is a warm 90 degrees and surrounded by bright colors, surfboard decor, and tiki
cabanas. You may even forget where you are!

Goldfish offers swim lessons for kids as young as 4 months old and hosts open
swim for families almost daily. For those looking for lessons, Goldfish recommends and offers "perpetual" swim lessons, billed monthly, allowing kids to have
an ongoing experience with the flexibility to change times, dates, or take time off
when needed. Classes have a 4:1 ratio of students to teachers.

Family Swim is open to the public for only $10 per person or $30 maximum
per family. Family Swim is scheduled on afternoons Monday through Saturday,
and evenings Friday and Saturday.

Insider tip: Find swim lessons that work for your family; Goldfish offers classes
once or twice a week, and drop-in classes are offered.

Cost: $10 per person or $30 per family for family swim.

Classes for ages 4 months to 12 years; family swim is for all ages.

Time to explore: 1 hour

Take CTA bus route #152 to Cumberland; Goldfish is just a short walk.

Free parking in lot.

KID'S ISLAND PLAY CAFÉ

2205 N. Southport Avenue, Chicago, IL 60614
(773) 935-6060
www.ChicagoKidsIsland.com
Monday–Friday 9:00 a.m.–6:00 p.m.; weekend hours dependent on party
schedule.

Children seem to have boundless energy, and chasing them around can be
exhausting, which is why a place like Kid's Island Play Café can be a blessing. It's a
great space to let the kids burn off some energy while parents relax and recharge
with some caffeine. Kid's Island Play Café is perfect for younger children, especially
toddlers and preschoolers. Ride-on toys, blocks, a play kitchen and market, and
many more toys are available, but the real showstopper is the indoor sandbox. Yes,
an indoor sandbox, complete with toys and a plastic slide. Parents will appreciate
the plush seats and free wifi. The café serves coffee and tea, pastries, children's
meals, sandwiches for adults, and snacks. Birthday party options are available.

LINCOLN PARK CONSERVATORY

2391 N. Stockton Drive, Chicago, IL 60614
(773) 883-7275
http://www.chicagoparkdistrict.com/parks/lincoln-park-conservatory/
Open 9:00 a.m.–5:00 p.m. daily

If you love lush grass, trees, and colorful flowers, then the Lincoln Park Conservatory is not to be missed. No matter the season outside, it's tropical in the four display houses—the Palm House, the Fern Room, the Orchid House, and the Show House—under the glass dome. In addition to plants and flowers, the conservatory is also home to tropical and koi fish in the ponds. Black thumbs to horticultural enthusiasts can all appreciate the Lincoln Park Conservatory for its variety of plants, including some very exotic orchids, educational information, and relaxation value. The Lincoln Park Conservatory hosts a Spring Flower Show and a Winter Train and Flower Show.

Next to the Conservatory is the Alfred Calder Lily Pond, a beautiful place to walk or relax in the spring or summer months. Just a short walk from Lincoln Park Zoo, the conservatory is perfect for a side trip before or after the zoo. Be sure to dress in layers, as it can be hot inside!

Insider tip: Watch out for dinosaurs! Tiny toy dinosaurs can be found among the plants in the gardens.

Free

Good for all ages.

Time to explore: 1–2 hours

Buses stop about a block away at Stockton and Webster and at Stockton and Fullerton.

Some street parking. Lot at Fullerton Parkway and Cannon is $20–$35.

LINCOLN PARK ZOO

2001 N. Clark Street, Chicago, IL 606014
(312) 742-2000
http://www.lpzoo.org
Open 10:00 a.m.–5:00 p.m. weekdays, 10:00 a.m.–6:30 p.m. weekends
Memorial Day through Labor Day, 10:00 a.m.–5:00 p.m. September–October,
10:00 a.m.–4:00 p.m. November–March, 10:00 a.m.–5:00 p.m. April–May.

Situated on 35 acres of beautifully landscaped property in the Lincoln Park
neighborhood, Lincoln Park Zoo is a Chicago treasure. Not only is it one of the
oldest zoos in the country, but it's also free. Don't let the admission price fool
you—Lincoln Park Zoo is filled with a huge variety of animals and exhibits. Native
wildlife including birds, turtles, fish, and frogs live along the Nature Boardwalk. If
more exotic animals pique your interest, there's the Primate House, Kovler Lion
House, Polar Bear and Penguin Habitat, or the Waterfowl Lagoon—just to name
a few! Lincoln Park Zoo's Farm-in-the-Zoo exhibit brings a farm to the city with
barnyard animals like cows, chickens, and goats. Visitors can also see farm equipment and learn about farming, including the milking process. For a few dollars,
take a ride on the Endangered Species Carousel or the Lionel Train Adventure.

In December and January Lincoln Park Zoo lights up the nights with Zoo Lights,
an impressive display of holiday lights throughout the zoo accompanied by special events and activities.

Insider tips: Get great skyline photos at the bridge over the South Pond. If you've
got younger kids, they'll definitely want some climbing time at the Pritzker Family
Children's Zoo Treetop Canopy.

Free. Lionel Train Adventure and Endangered Species Carousel are $3 each
per person.

Good for all ages.

Time to explore: 3–5 hours

Brown and Purple lines at Armitage Station one mile west. CTA buses #151 and
#156 at West Gate or Farm in Zoo. CTA bus #22 at West Gate and Brauer Gate.

Some street parking. Lot on Fullerton Parkway and Cannon is $20–$35.

MARGARET DONAHUE PARK

1230 W. School Street, Chicago, IL 60657
(312) 742-7826
http://www.chicagoparkdistrict.com/parks/margaret-donahue-park/
Open 6:00 a.m.–11:00 p.m. daily.

The Cubs play at Wrigley Field, but now your little cubs can play on the Cubs field less than a mile away at Margaret Donahue Park. The playground, which has a play structure that resembles buildings in the Chicago skyline, has swings, a large climbing web, slides, a climbing wall, and plenty of rubberized hills. There are canopy-covered tables nearby from which parents can observe or for picnicking. The playground is gated and has a rubberized surface for safety. There's also a splash pad for kids to frolic in during the summer.

Insider tip: The shade here is limited, so don't forget the sun protection, and keep in mind there are no bathrooms available.
Free
Designed for kids 4 to 8 years old.
Time to explore: 1–2 hours
Take Brown Line train to Southport, a few blocks from the park.
Street parking is available.

OZ PARK

2021 N. Burling Street, Chicago, IL 60614
(312) 742-7898
http://www.chicagoparkdistrict.com/parks/Oz-Park/
6:00 a.m.–11:00 p.m. daily

Who knew you could find Oz right here in Chicago? No tornadoes needed to make the journey—there's plenty of parking and public transportation. Oz Park pays tribute to L. Frank Baum, author of the Oz series of books, with statues of Dorothy (complete with ruby red slippers) and Toto, the Tin Man, the Scarecrow, and the Cowardly Lion. Little known fact: L. Frank Baum was actually living right here in the merry old land of Chicago when he wrote *The Wonderful Wizard of Oz*. Visitors can enjoy the blooms in the community garden, aptly named the Emerald City Garden, and kids will love Dorothy's Playlot, with a large wooden play structure that resembles a castle. Sadly, you won't find a yellow brick road here.

Insider tip: Bring your little dog, too—Oz Park is pet-friendly.
Free
Good for all ages.
Time to explore: 1–2 hours
Brown and Purple Lines at Armitage half a mile away. CTA bus routes #11, #37, and #74 stop at Webster and Orchard; CTA bus route #8 at Halsted and Dickens.
Free street parking.

PEGGY NOTEBAERT NATURE CENTER

2430 N. Cannon Drive, Chicago, IL 60614
(773) 755-5100
www.naturemuseum.org
Open 9:00 a.m.–5:00 p.m. Monday through Friday, 10:00 a.m.–5:00 p.m.
Saturday and Sunday. Open 362 days a year; closed on the first Friday in May,
Thanksgiving, and Christmas.

Explore an Extreme Greenhouse, learn about the Mysteries of the Marsh,
and test out RiverWorks while splashing in the water table at the Peggy Note-
baert Nature Museum. You can also visit the Judy Istock Butterfly Haven, a
2,700-square-foot greenhouse with more than 40 species of exotic butterflies.

The Hands On Habitat is for the smallest environmental explorers, and they
can play around in a submarine, explore a cave, and climb a spider's web. Toddlers and preschoolers will probably be happy to spend the entire day there, so
if you want to see the rest of the nature center, you might want to make this the
last stop.

There's a gift shop and café, and you can bring your own food. If the weather
is nice, you can view birds and the skyline through binoculars on the birdwalk or
explore the nature trails.

Insider tip: The Judy Istock Butterfly Haven is one
of the most beautiful and relaxing places in the
city—do not miss it.

Admission is $9 per adult; children ages 3–12 are
$6. Thursdays are suggested donation days for
Illinois residents.

Best for toddlers and up.

Time to explore: 3–4 hours

CTA bus routes #76, #151, and #156 stop at the
museum.

Free street parking is available, but sometimes
limited. If you can't find free parking, there is a
parking lot nearby that will cost you $20–$35.

PICKLE'S PLAYROOM

2315 W. Lawrence Avenue, Chicago, IL 60625
(773) 293-7747
www.picklesplayroom.net
Open 9:00 a.m.–5:00 p.m. Monday–Friday, 9:00 a.m.–3:30 p.m.
Saturday, 8:00 a.m.–12:30 p.m. Sunday.

Being a parent means multitasking, and places like Pickle's Playroom make it
easy and fun, allowing you to cross haircut, lunch, and active time for the kids off
the to-do list without whining from the kids. Pickle's Playroom has a full salon,
complete with fun seats for little ones. They offer haircuts and manicures for

children and adults, and even trendy services like hair chalking.

Right under the same roof is the playroom and café, where kids can climb the play structure, slide down the slide, and play with trains or dolls while parents keep an eye on them from nearby chairs. Crawlers have their own area, and Pickle's serves sandwiches and salads in the café. Socks are required in the play area (for children and adults) and Pickle's also has classes and hosts birthday parties.

Insider tip: Pickle's Playroom has its own digital family radio station. Drop by on Wednesday morning to attend their radio party from 10:00 a.m. to 11:00 a.m., with music, dancing, and activities for kids and their parents.

Playroom cost is $12 for crawlers and up for 2 hours, $9 for a sibling. Haircuts for children start at about $20 and include 30 minutes of playtime.

Designed for children ages 6 months–7 years (for playroom); salon serves all ages.

Time to explore: 1–2 hours

Take Brown Line train to Western stop; Pickle's Playroom is just a short walk away.

Free street parking and pay box lot.

PURPLE MONKEY PLAYROOM
2040 N. Western Avenue, Chicago, IL 60647
(773) 772-8411
www.purplemonkeyplayroom.com
Monday–Friday 9:30 a.m.–5:30 p.m., weekend drop-in hours dependent upon party schedule.

Welcome to the jungle, baby! Purple Monkey Playroom is the perfect place to take your little monkeys to play. Painted with trees and monkeys, Purple Monkey Playroom is bright and playful and filled with tons of fun stuff—dress-up clothes, a slide, a tiki hut, train table, play kitchen, and lots more. There's a separate area for crawlers, and you can save money on multiple visits by purchasing a 5- or 10-visit pass or monthly or annual unlimited membership. Parents can take a seat in cushy chairs right there in the playroom, so it's easy to keep an eye on the kids and enjoy free coffee, tea, and wifi. Outside food is allowed in, and socks are required. Purple Monkey Playroom also offers supervised drop-off playtime in partnership with Sittercity, and they have classes, including Spanish and Chinese, for kids as young as 6 months old.

Insider tip: Admission is good for a full day of play, so you and your child(ren) can leave and return—great if you need to run out to a restaurant or leave for a nap.

$15 per child. 0–7 months $7 or free with paid sibling. Each additional sibling is $3.

Best for children 6 months through 5 years old.

Time to explore: 2–3 hours

Many CTA bus stops nearby on Western and on Milwaukee and Armitage. Blue Line at Western a couple blocks away.

Free parking in lot and on street.

SPECTRUM TOY STORE

1911 W. Belmont, Chicago, IL 60657
(773) 231-8001
www.spectrumtoystore.com
Open 10:00 a.m.–7:00 p.m. Monday–Friday, 9:00 a.m.–7:00 p.m. Saturday,
10:00 a.m.–6:00 p.m. Sunday

Spectrum Toy Store has colorful toys in the window and looks like a typical toy store; however, it's anything but that. Spectrum is unique because it's the only toy store in the state (and one of the few in the United States) specifically for children with developmental disabilities. Spectrum is a program of the non-profit CARE Foundation, which provides services and programs for children with disabilities and their families, and is owned by a behavioral therapist. Parents and children can see, feel, and play with toys before buying so they can decide what works for them. Spectrum isn't just about toys either—they also sell special needs products and adaptive equipment.

Insider tip: Spectrum also offers daily programs and support groups.
Call for details.

Free to browse

Focused on children ages 3 to 13 years old.

Time to explore: 1 hour or less

Take CTA bus route #77 to the Belmont and Wolcott stop just outside Spectrum.
Street parking is available.

WHIRLYBALL

1825 W. Webster, Chicago, IL 60614
(773) 486-7777
www.whirlyball.com/location-chicago/
Open 11:00 a.m.–midnight Sunday–Thursday, 11:00 a.m.–2:00 a.m.
Friday, 11:00 a.m.–3:00 a.m. Saturday.

Imagine playing a combination of basketball and lacrosse with high-speed bumper cars. If you think it sounds painful—well, you're right, but it's also a lot of fun. WhirlyBall isn't for little ones—participants must be at least 4'6" to play—but older kids and adults will love it.

WhirlyBall isn't all that's here; it's a full sports bar with video games, air hockey, foosball, pool tables, plus bowling (aka "WhirlyBowl") and laser tag. The menu includes sophisticated bar food like fig bruschetta, craft pizzas, and macaroni and cheese with truffle oil. There are additional locations in Lombard and Vernon Hills.

Insider tip: WhirlyBall is even better in a large group, so schedule a party or event with friends.

Cost: $15 per player (minimum 4). Walk in or court rental. 4' 6" to play. WhirlyBowl $10–$15 per hour. $4 shoe rental. Laser tag (ages 8+) $15/player (minimum 4).

Best for ages 8 and up.

Time to explore: 2–4 hours

Near Metra's Clybourn station and CTA train and bus stop at Elston and Webster.

Parking is available on the street and in lot.

Sports

CHICAGO CUBS
Wrigley Field, 1060 W. Addison Street, Chicago, IL 60613
(773) 404-2827
http://chicago.cubs.mlb.com/
Season runs from April to October.

You may not have heard since it wasn't publicized much, but the Chicago Cubs won the 2016 World Series after a 108-year drought. The Cubs were the team with the dubious distinction of having the longest streak between World Series wins, but that only made their fans more dedicated to cheering them on to victory. Because Chicago has two baseball teams—the Cubs and the White Sox—there tends to be a rivalry between fans of each team, but the North Side belongs to the Cubs.

Despite the long drought, the Chicago Cubs have had some outstanding players through the years, from Ryne Sandberg to Sammy Sosa to Kerry Wood. Some of the most famous Cubs are represented by statues outside the stadium—Hall of Famers Billy Williams, Ernie Banks, and Ron Santo, and Cubs broadcaster and superfan Harry Carey. Arrive early for the game and hang out by the Club Box wall for a chance to get autographs from current coaches and players; fans are allowed to be there for autographs from the time the gates open until batting practice cages are removed before the game.

The Cubs love kids and have fan clubs specifically for children. Pay a fee to sign a child up for the Newborn Fan Club, and receive a Cubs onesie and other memorabilia. Older kids can sign up for Clark's Crew. There is a fee for the respective clubs, but kids receive memorabilia and special fan club benefits. Sunday games are Kids Sundays and the first 1,000 children under the age of 13 receive a wristband that allows them to run the bases with Cubs mascot Clark the Cub.

Wrigley Field, built in 1914 and home to the Cubs for 100 years, is an attraction by itself and tours are offered so you can see what you don't see when you attend a game. Tours are offered on select days (see website for schedule) and last about 75–90 minutes. Dress for the weather because much of the tour is outdoors, and you'll walk about a mile. Tour tickets are $25 per person and children under 2 are free. Tours are offered on both game days and non-game days, but the areas you see will differ depending on whether it's a game day or not.

Insider tip: If your child is attending his/her first Cubs game, stop by the First Timer's desk in the main concourse near Gate D to pick up an official First Timer's certificate.

Ticket prices for 2017 haven't been announced yet, but expect them to go up from previous years now that the Cubs are World Series champs. Children 2 and under do not need a ticket if they sit on a parent's lap.

Games usually last about 3 hours.

CTA Red Line train stops at the Wrigley Field Addison station; CTA bus routes #22 and #152 stop at Clark and Addison.

Free remote parking is available at 3900 N. Rockwell Street with a free shuttle to the field.

Restaurants

CAFÉ BA-BA-REEBA

2024 N. Halsted Street, Chicago, IL 60614
(773) 935-5000
www.CafeBaBaReeba.com
Open for brunch on Saturday and Sunday, and lunch and dinner daily.

Sometimes a meal is more than just food; it's an adventure. That's what you can expect at Café Ba-Ba-Reeba. Spanish tapas, paella, and sangria are on the menu at this lively restaurant that is just loud enough that you don't have to worry about your kids causing a scene. The beauty of tapas is that it's small plates to be shared, so you get to sample lots of different things, like garlic potato salad, artisanal cheeses, skewered chicken and chorizo sausage, and beef empanadas. Gluten-free dishes are also available.

Kids receive crayons and Wikki Stix to entertain them. Need more of something? You can continue to order additional plates as needed throughout your meal. Kids' meals come with carrots and hummus as an appetizer and fruit for dessert. Everything on the dessert menu is only $3, just the right price for sampling and sharing around the table. Picky kids and budding foodies alike will all be pleased.

Kids' meals are $5–$7. Small plates range in price from about $4 to $20.

CTA bus route #8 stops at Halsted and Dickens, and bus route #73 stops at Armitage and Fremont. Brown and Purple Line trains stop at the Armitage stop about a half mile away.

Some street parking available. Valet parking is available for $13.

MON AMI GABI

2300 N. Lincoln Park West, Chicago, IL 60614
(773) 348-8886
www.monamigabi.com
Open for dinner daily and brunch on Sunday.

Mon Ami Gabi is a classic Parisian bistro with an elegant dining room and outdoor patio seating, which sounds wonderful for a date, but it's also surprisingly kid-friendly.

Mon Ami Gabi serves brunch on Sundays, with a variety of sweet and savory options; kids can order things like crème brûlée French toast and bananas foster waffles. For dinner, adults can choose from steak, seafood, and poultry dishes. The kids' menu includes an appetizer of baby carrots and dip, and a choice of things like grilled cheese, pasta, chicken, or steak, all served on compartmentalized dishes.

Reservations are recommended.

Kids' meals range from about $4 to $12; adult entrees are about $12–$40.

CTA bus routes #22 and #36 stop at Clark and Belden, and routes #151 and #156 stop on Stockton at Webster and at Fullerton, within a few blocks of Mon Ami Gabi.

Street and valet parking available.

PALM COURT AT THE DRAKE

The Drake Hotel, 140 E. Walton Place, Chicago, IL 60611
(312) 787-2200
www.thedrakehotel.com/dining/palm-court
Seatings every hour and a half between 1:00 p.m. and 5:00 p.m.

Everyone likes to dress up for a fancy outing every once in a while, and after-noon tea at Palm Court is the perfect occasion. Settle into the impressive and el-egant Palm Court, with a beautiful indoor fountain, chandeliers, and plush seats, and choose from a large selection of flavored teas. As you begin to sip your tea, a tiered tea tray will arrive with an assortment of savory finger sandwiches, petit fours, and pastries with preserves, lemon curd, and Devon cream. Children between 4 and 12 years old can enjoy the "Little Prince and Princess Tea" and substitute hot chocolate or a kiddie cocktail for tea and have Nutella and jelly finger sandwiches added to the tea tray. Vegetarian and gluten-free diets can be accommodated as well.

Insider tip: Afternoon tea includes refills, so go ahead and ask for more finger sandwiches or pastries if you start to run low.

$49 for adults, $24 for kids.

CTA bus route #151 stops at Michigan and Oak.

Valet parking is about $70, self-park $48.

PARACHUTE

3500 N. Elston Avenue, Chicago, IL 60618
(773) 654-1460
www.parachuterestaurant.com
Open for dinner Tuesday through Saturday; closed Sunday and Monday.

Mac and cheese and burgers are kid favorites, but everybody needs a change sometimes. Parachute is a small, 40-seat restaurant in the Avondale neighbor-hood serving small plates of Korean American food. There's no mac and cheese on the Parachute kids' menu, but there are traditional Korean dishes with a twist. Each kids' meal is served with fruit, miso soup, roasted seaweed, and house Kimchi.

The menu changes daily based on products at their peak and availability, so there are always opportunities to try new dishes.

Families with children are encouraged to visit earlier in the evening, between 5:00 p.m. and 6:00 p.m., when the restaurant is not as busy. Bonus: there's a park across the street.

Dishes are about $10–$25; they are designed for diners to order multiple dishes to share.

Ten-minute walk from the Belmont Blue Line.

Free street parking.

SUPERDAWG

6363 N. Milwaukee Avenue, Chicago, IL 60646
(773) 763-0660
www.Superdawg.com
Sunday–Thursday 11:00 a.m.–1:00 a.m., Friday–Saturday 11:00 a.m.–2:00 a.m.

A trip to Chicago isn't complete without a Chicago dog, so make your way to Superdawg, where they're serving up dogs and nostalgia. Two giant hot dogs— Mr. and Mrs. Superdawg—stand on top of the roof of this Chicago landmark, where you can dine inside or have a car hop bring your food right to your window. The Superdawg is a juicy pure beef hot dog on a poppy seed bun, topped with mustard, piccalilli, chopped onions, a dill pickle, and a hot pepper, and it's served with a batch of crinkle-cut french fries. Besides hot dogs, Superdawg has the Superburger, Supercheese, malts, shakes, sundaes, and the Whoopsidawg, a combination of Romanian and Hungarian Polish sausage on a roll topped with a special sauce, grilled onion, and a pickle. Wanna make your friends jealous? Snag a souvenir Superdawg t-shirt or keychain. There is an additional Superdawg location in Wheeling at 333 S. Milwaukee Avenue.

A meal will cost about $10.

CTA bus route #86 and Pace route #270 stop at Milwaukee and Nagle.

Free parking in the lot.

Free Activities

- **Lincoln Park Zoo**—Lions and tigers and bears, oh my! See them all (and lots more).

- **Lincoln Park Conservatory**—It's green and lush (and free!) year-round at the Lincoln Park Conservatory.

- **Alfred Caldwell Lily Pond**—Take a walk or just sit and enjoy the beautiful landscape.

- **Oz Park**—Don your ruby slippers and take a trip to the merry old land of Oz Park, where you can pose with statues of your favorite Wizard of Oz characters and play in "Dorothy's Playlot."

- **Foster Beach**—Head east for a splash in the lake at any of Chicago's beaches. Foster Beach is particularly family-friendly, with restrooms, showers, and concessions available.

- **The 606**—Stretch your legs with a walk or ride along the trails at this new park and trail system in Logan Square.

- **DePaul University Art Museum**—Put art appreciation on your agenda with a visit to this museum in Lincoln Park. Check their calendar for family-friendly events.

- **North Park Village Nature Center**—There's more than skyscrapers in Chicago—like 46 acres of nature preserve including woodlands, wetlands, prairie, savanna, and an educational center.

- **Green City Market**—Get some fresh air and fresh fruits, veggies, and flowers, or just enjoy some people-watching.

✳ WEST/NEAR WEST ✳

The West Side of Chicago is a working-class area—home to many with cultural institutions and ethnic restaurants. Two large annual events occur here: Fiestas Puertorriquenas in Humboldt Park in the early summer and Festa Italiana in Little Italy celebrated in late summer. The Illinois Medical District is located in this area, as is the Cook County Jail, the largest jail in the country, covering 96 acres. Public transportation is plentiful, with a large number of bus routes and the Blue, Green, and Pink train lines serving the area. Driving is convenient too, as the Eisenhower expressway (also known as 290) runs through the West Side.

Attractions

ADVENTURE STAGE
Vittum Theater, 1012 N. Noble Street, Chicago, IL 60642
(773) 342-4141
www.adventurestage.org
Show times vary.

Adventure Stage is a nonprofit organization dedicated to creating and telling heroic stories about young people. Shows staged by Adventure Stage are designed for children and teens from about 8 to 14 years old and tell stories like that of a young boy leaving his homeland for America and trying to assimilate to his new home, or of teens attempting to discover who they are despite peer pressure and bullying. The Vittum Theater is small, holding only 299 people, and there's no such thing as a bad seat here.

Adventure Stage also offers classroom and community programs. Young artists (ages 11–15) are encouraged to get involved with Adventure Stage to work with theater professionals to help bring personal stories to the stage. Young playwrights are invited to enter a nationwide contest. Details for these opportunities can be found on their website.

Insider tip: Arrive early for pre-show audience questions. There are also post-show curtain talks.

Tickets are $17/adult, $12/child (14 and under).

Designed for ages 8 to 14.

Show lengths vary; be sure to add in time for pre- and post-show discussions.

CTA bus #56 at Milwaukee and Noble. Blue Line at Milwaukee and Ashland half a mile away.

Free and metered street parking.

BIG MONSTER DOOR

21 S. Racine Avenue, Chicago, IL 60607
No phone number
Visit during daylight hours.

You'll see a lot of doors along Racine Avenue for apartments, businesses, a former police station—but one door in particular stands out because it's more than twice the size of all the rest. Big Monster Toys isn't open to the public, but maybe that's a good thing because they have a giant monster inside!

See if you can reach the doorknob or wave to the monster (who's more funny-looking than scary), and be sure you have a camera with you, because this is a great spot for some fun photos with the kids.

Insider tip: Don't forget the camera and take lots of photos; this is a great backdrop for a Christmas card, family photo, or just some fun snapshots to frame and hang.

Free

Good for all ages.

Time to explore: Less than 1 hour

CTA bus route #20 stops at Madison and Racine.

Free street parking.

CHICAGO CHILDREN'S THEATRE

The Station, 100 S. Racine Avenue, Chicago, IL 60607
(773) 227-0180
www.chicagochildrenstheatre.org
Show times vary. Performances are offered weekdays and weekends in the mornings, afternoons, and evenings.

In a time when TVs, computers, tablets, and cell phones are constantly available to entertain even the smallest children, seeing a live performance at the Chicago Children's Theatre can be absolutely magical. The Chicago Children's Theatre is the largest professional theater company dedicated to shows for children, and their professionalism always shows in their performances.

Whether the performance is based on an unfamiliar feature or well-known stories like Brown Bear, Brown Bear by Eric Carle or Pinocchio, the show will be new and exciting. The Chicago Children's Theatre uses lighting, sound, props, costumes, and an unmatched level of artistry to create entire worlds for each show. Although the shows are made especially for children, they are not just children's shows; they are artistic productions that will enchant the audience, regardless of age.

The Chicago Children's Theatre serves low-income families by offering thousands of free tickets to the Chicago Public Schools each season. They also serve children with special needs through the Red Kite Project, which offers theater experiences for children on the autism spectrum and for children with hearing or vision impairments or Down Syndrome.

After performing at a few different locations over the years, the Chicago Children's Theatre has its own home as of 2017, allowing it to conduct classes and camps, theater performances, and family experiences all under one roof.

Insider tip: The Chicago Children's Theatre's new location is about two blocks from the Big Monster Door, so be sure you check that out too.

Ticket prices vary, but expect to pay about $25–$40 per ticket. Savings of up to 75% are available when you purchase a subscription pass for multiple shows.

Age recommendations vary according to the show; there are shows for all ages—toddlers, grade schoolers, and tweens.

Show length varies, but most shows are about 1 hour.

CTA bus route #20 stops at Madison and Racine a few blocks away.

Limited parking is available in the building's parking lot and street parking is available.

CHIC-A-GO-GO

CAN-TV, 1309 S. Wood Street, Chicago, IL 60608
(312) 738-1400
http://cantv.org/about-us/about-can-tv/
http://www.roctober.com/chicagogo/

CAN-TV public access TV center is the home of *Chic-A-Go-Go*, a quirky all-ages dance TV show similar to *Soul Train* or *American Bandstand*, and it's a fun and unique experience to share with your family. *Chic-A-Go-Go* premiered in 1996 and is televised on cable Channel 19 on Tuesdays at 8:30 p.m. and Wednesdays at 3:30 p.m. Music is the centerpiece of the show—music is played for dancing and each episode includes a performance by musicians. Artists are interviewed by the host, Ratso, a teenage rat puppet, and each show concludes with the "El Train Line" (like *Soul Train*'s parallel line of dancers with couples doing their own thing down the middle of the two lines.)

Check out the website or Facebook page (www.facebook.com/chicagogo), or sign up for their email newsletter to be notified of filming dates and times. Dress cute or crazy—you'll see it all there—and get ready for your moment of fame. Who knows? Maybe you'll be discovered!

Tip: Warm up your dance moves and wear some comfy shoes, because you'll be cutting a rug.

Free

Good for all ages.

Time to explore: 1–3 hours

CAN-TV has a parking lot and metered parking is available nearby.

The Polk stop of the Pink Line is half a mile away.

GARFIELD PARK CONSERVATORY

300 N. Central Park, Chicago, IL 60624
(312) 746-5100
www.garfieldconservatory.org
Thursday–Tuesday 9:00 a.m.–5:00 p.m., Wednesday 9:00 a.m.–8:00 p.m.

A tropical vacation might not be possible when you have little ones, but taking them to a tropical environment is. The Garfield Park Conservatory is free and lets you enjoy all the beauty of nature indoors. The Conservatory, which is run by the Chicago Park District and located in the Garfield Park neighborhood, is more than a century old and is one of the largest conservatories in the country. Experience different climates as well as trees, plants, and flowers as you stroll through all the areas of the Conservatory, including the Desert Room, Aroid House, and Palm House. See what prehistoric Chicago looked like in the Fern House, and learn about how plants create energy in the Sugar from the Sun room. The Show House, where flowers are grown for annual flower shows, is beautiful and provides an excellent backdrop for photos. The Elizabeth Morse Children's Garden is a large garden/playroom for kids with a platform to view the garden from above, a vine tube slide, and a giant seed to explore. There is also a small play area for babies and toddlers.

With two acres inside and 12 acres outside (open in the summer), you could easily spend a few hours exploring and playing. Pack a lunch and enjoy a picnic in the outdoor gardens, or eat at one of the tables in Horticulture Hall. If you prefer to go to a restaurant for dinner, Inspiration Kitchen is just around the corner and is open Wednesday through Saturday.

Visit on Mondays between 10:00 a.m. and noon for Morning Glories; the Elizabeth Morse Children's Garden will have opportunities for kids to dig in soil, listen to stories, and work on projects. The Children's Garden also has Plant Party Play Dates on weekends.

Insider tip: Dress in layers. You'll be moving between hot and cool environments, so layers will make the visit much more pleasant.

Free. Donations are accepted.

Good for all ages.

Time to explore: 1–3 hours

CTA Green Line to Conservatory/Central Park Drive Station.

Parking lot with free parking.

KID CITY

1837 W. Grand Avenue, Chicago, IL 60622
(312) 967-9269
www.kidcitychicago.com
Monday–Friday 9:30 a.m.–6:00 p.m. (October through April), 9:30 a.m.–4:30 p.m. (May through September). Weekends hours are dependent on party schedule.

Kid City is a spacious, colorful indoor play space where kids can get some energy out and parents can enjoy coffee while relaxing. Dress-up clothes, puzzles, ride-on toys, a playhouse, a play kitchen, and a grocery store are just a few of the things Kid City has to offer in the 3,000-square-foot space, and they have a separate area for crawlers. Coffee is free and there's a parents' lounge with comfortable sofas. Bring lunch or a snack—outside food is allowed, but they do not allow any nut products. Don't forget socks! They're a must, but if you do forget, you can purchase them for $2.

Kid City offers party packages, drop-off camps, and special events. Multi-visit passes and memberships are available.

Insider tip: Strollers aren't allowed. They do have an area at the front where you can park them, but if you have an infant, you might want to have a baby carrier for use while you visit.

$15 for the first child, with discounts for siblings. Noncrawlers without siblings are $6.

Recommended for children ages 6 months through 6 years and their caregivers.

Time to explore: 1–2 hours

CTA bus 65 within a block at Grand and Wood. Green and Pink Lines stop at Ashland about half a mile away.

Free parking on Grand Avenue.

NATIONAL MUSEUM OF MEXICAN ART

1853 W. 19th Street, Chicago, IL 60608
(312) 738-1503
http://www.nationalmuseumofmexicanart.org
Tuesday–Sunday 10:00 a.m.–5:00 p.m.; closed Mondays

The National Museum of Mexican Art, a non-profit museum located in Pilsen, has a collection of more than 10,000 pieces, including textiles, folk art, photography, print and drawings, paintings, sculptures, and more, documenting 3,000 years of creativity. With one of the largest permanent collections in the country, the National Museum of Mexican Art strives to preserve and stimulate knowledge of Mexican culture. Their permanent exhibit, *Nuestras Historias,* features works from the permanent collection to tell the story of the constantly evolving Mexican identity in the United States. They also offer a wide range of temporary exhibits.

The National Museum of Mexican Art also offers adult and child classes, including after-school and weekend art classes, a bilingual summer camp, and a variety of cultural programs throughout the year. Family Sunday is offered from noon to 2:00 p.m., with gallery tours and opportunities to create art for kids 4 to 12 years old.

Insider tip: The National Museum of Mexican Art hosts a *Dia de los Muertos* (Day of the Dead) celebration annually in the fall that's definitely worth checking out.

Free

Best for ages 4 and up.

Time to explore: 1–2 hours

Take the Pink Line to Damen or 18th Street, or CTA bus route #50 Damen to 19th Street, or bus route #9 Ashland to 18th Street.

Street parking.

PILSEN MURALS

Primarily in the Pilsen neighborhood of Chicago; in the area bordered by 16th Street, Western Avenue, and the Chicago River.

Daylight hours

Not all art can be found in galleries; sometimes it's right there in front of us just waiting to be discovered, and this is especially true in Pilsen.

The Pilsen neighborhood of Chicago is primarily a Mexican-American neighborhood with a long history of being home to immigrants. As a celebration of the rich culture of Pilsen, the Chicago Urban Art Society worked to display murals created by internationally recognized artists. There are murals of all kinds throughout the Pilsen area, representing a variety of themes and techniques, but many depict images related to migration, gentrification, and religion. Some of the most well-known murals are Francisco Mendoza's glass tile mosaic at Orozco Community Academy, 1645 W. 18th Avenue, Jeff Zimmerman's *Increíbles Las Cosas Q' Se Ven* at 19th and Ashland, and the mural at the Pink Line station at 18th Street.

Insider tip: Plan on visiting the National Museum of Mexican Art, located in Pilsen, during your trip.

Free

Good for all ages.

Time to explore: 1–3 hours

Public transportation depends on where you begin and end your trip; there are many bus routes in the area and the Pink and Blue lines have several stops in the area.

Street parking is available in Pilsen.

Sports

CHICAGO BLACKHAWKS

United Center, 1901 W. Madison Street, Chicago, IL
(312) 455-7000
www.Blackhawks.nhl.com
Season runs October through April

The excitement builds as the players line up, the puck is dropped, and THWAP—the game is on! Hockey is a fast, physical, intense game, and the Chicago Blackhawks are champions, winning the Stanley Cup in 2010, 2013, and 2015. Kids can become part of mascot TommyHawk's "Tommy's Crew" fan club. Memberships are $20–$40 depending on the benefits offered. Outside the United Center, check out statues honoring hockey greats Bobby Hull and Stan Mikita.

Tickets go on sale in mid-August, and it's best to buy them early. Children under 3 do not need a ticket if they are sitting on a parent's lap. Family restrooms are available at Level 100 across from 115/116 in the First Aid Room and at the top of Section 303/304.

Aside from games, the Blackhawks offer a reading program for K–8 schools in the Chicagoland area, giving students the opportunity to win special prizes. They also host free Outdoor Clinics in Chicago parks. Prior skating experience and registration is required. The use of skates and equipment is free and each participating child receives a jersey to keep.

If games are too expensive or sold out, see the Blackhawks practice for free on select dates (see website) at Johnny's IceHouse West. Autographs are not allowed before or after practice sessions.

Tickets start at about $50 and go up from there.

Games usually last about two and a half hours.

Take the Orange, Green, Purple, and Brown lines to Madison, and then the #20 Madison bus west. There is also a #19 United Center Express Bus on game days (starting 90 minutes prior to the game).

Parking is $22–$29 in the lots.

CHICAGO BULLS

United Center, 1901 W. Madison Street, Chicago, IL 60612
(312) 455-4000
www.nba.com/bulls
Season runs October through April

Chicago is and has been home to myriad celebrities, with Michael Jordan right at the top of the list. Jordan spent 14 years playing for the Chicago Bulls, and the team won six NBA Championships during that time. Now you can see Jordan's successors, including Dwayne Wade, Rajon Rondo, and Jimmy Butler, play hoops at the United Center from October through April.

The Chicago Bulls have many opportunities for kids to get involved and even appear at games, including the Bullskidz dance group for boys and girls ages 7–12, the Jr. Luvabulls for girls between the ages of 5 and 18, and the Ballboy/Ballgirl program for teens between 16 and 20 years old.

A 12-foot-tall statue of Michael Jordan about to dunk used to sit outside the United Center, but it was recently moved inside and will now be on display in the new United Center atrium.

Tickets start at about $45. Children under 36 inches do not need a ticket if they sit on a parent's lap.

Take the Orange, Green, Purple, and Brown lines to Madison, and then the #20 Madison bus west. There is also a #19 United Center Express Bus on game days (starting 90 minutes prior to the game).

There are parking lots on all sides of the United Center and parking costs $24–$40.

WINDY CITY ROLLERS

UIC Pavilion, 525 S. Racine, Chicago, IL 60607
UIC Pavilion (312) 413-5740
www.windycityrollers.com
Season runs April through October

Roller derby doesn't exactly seem like a warm and fuzzy family activity, but it is surprisingly family-friendly. The Windy City Rollers is an all-female flat-track Chicago roller derby league with four league teams—Double Crossers, The Fury, Hell's Belles, and Manic Attackers—as well as two travel teams—Windy City Roller's All-Star Team and Second Wind—and a farm team called Haymarket Rioters.

The game is aggressive, as are many of the skaters' names, but it's all in good fun, and they make a strong effort to be welcoming and inclusive to the spectators. Skaters are often in the stands or walking through the stadium to talk to fans and sign autographs.

If you don't know much about the sport of roller derby, you can learn about it in the "How to Watch" video on their website, and they do a demonstration before the game. Kids are invited down to the track as players are announced so they can high-five the skaters as they make their entrance. Merchandise and concessions are available for purchase, and because it's a large venue you won't be cramped in your seat; there is often plenty of room to change seats or let the kids stretch their legs during the game.

Tickets start at about $15.

The Racine Blue Line stop is across the street; CTA bus routes #7, #60, and #755 also go to the UIC Pavilion.

Parking is about $15.

Restaurants

ORIGINAL FERRARA BAKERY

2210 W. Taylor Street, Chicago, IL 60612
(312) 666-2800
http://www.ferrarabakery.com
Monday–Friday 8:30 a.m.–4:30 p.m., Saturday 9:00 a.m.–4:00 p.m., Sunday
10:00 a.m.–2:00 p.m. Lunch is served Monday through Friday, and a limited
lunch menu on Saturday. Lunch is not served on Sunday.

It's usually a good sign when "original" is included in the name of the restaurant. The Original Ferrara Bakery is family owned and has been around since 1908. The interior is warm and friendly, with several tables. Although the focus is still cakes and pastries, they've expanded to include a lunch menu. Eggplant Parmigiana, Shells Primavera, the Ferrara Signature cold Italian sandwich, Chili Toscani, and Caprese salad are just a few of the options they offer. There's no kids' menu, but the prices are really reasonable, and you can purchase a side order of pasta for less than $4.

It can't be stressed enough—do not miss out on the desserts. Cannolis, Italian cookies, créme puffs, eclairs, napoleons, zeppole, tiramisu, and many other delicious desserts fill the cases here, and they are fantastic. The Ferrara family knows how to do sweets—they also own the Ferrara Pan Candy Company in Forest Park, famous for making candies such as Lemonheads and Atomic Fireballs.

Lunches are around $7–$8.
CTA bus route #157 stops at Ogden and Taylor.
Metered street parking is available.

GREEK ISLANDS

200 S. Halsted Street, Chicago, IL 60661
(312) 782-9855
http://www.greekislands.net
Sunday–Thursday 11:00 a.m.–midnight, Friday–Saturday 11:00 a.m.–1:00 a.m.

A meal at Greek Islands isn't just about food, it's also about the experience. Cobblestone floors and Parthenon-themed decor give it a lively and homey feel and prepare you for your culinary adventure. Greek Islands has been creating authentic Greek meals since 1971, shipping in extra virgin olive oil, wines, cheeses, herbs, and seafood from Greece. The very extensive menu includes mouthwatering dishes like grilled octopus, spanakotiropita, gyros, roast loin of lamb, and kabobs, and they have a kids' menu. A really good bet is the Family Feast, which includes appetizers, salad, four different entrees, a side dish, and dessert for less than $25 per person. There are also plenty of vegetarian and gluten-free options for those on restricted diets.

Greek Islands is billed as "America's Most Popular Greek Restaurant," and Chicagoans and visitors alike love it. Reservations are not required, but they're definitely a good idea. There is an additional location in Lombard.

Most entrees are in the $10–$20 range.

CTA bus route #126 stops at Van Buren and Halsted, a couple blocks away. Union Station is about half a mile away.

Street parking. Greek Islands sometimes offers free valet service.

GREEN TOMATO CAFÉ

3750 W. Ogden Avenue, Chicago, IL 60623
(872) 588-3380
www.GreenTomatoCafe.org
Open for breakfast and lunch Monday through Saturday. Closed Sunday. Kitchen closes at 4:00 p.m. on weekdays; coffee, smoothies, soup, salads, and sandwiches are available until 8:00 p.m.

When Lawndale Christian Health Center officials decided to provide its Health and Fitness Center patients and employees with a place nearby to purchase healthy food, they resolved that the community should benefit as well and opened the Green Tomato Café. Healthy salads, sandwiches, and smoothies are made fresh from scratch with locally sourced ingredients. The result is a tasty menu of affordable breakfast, lunch, and dinner items, as well as locally ground coffee. Green Tomato Café isn't just a place to eat, but also a great place to meet up with friends. With wooden benches and tables, Green Tomato Café has just the right seating for a small family or a playdate get-together. They have a lounge area with comfortable couches and free wifi, and a special area just for the kids with small tables and chairs and some toys.

Cost: under $10.

Short walk from the Central Park or Pulaski-Cermak stop of the Pink Line.

Street and lot parking.

INSPIRATION KITCHEN

3504 W. Lake Street, Chicago, IL 60624
(773) 801-1110
www.InspirationKitchens.org
Closed Monday and Tuesday. Open for lunch and dinner Wednesday–Friday, brunch and dinner Saturday, and brunch on Sunday.

Inspiration Kitchen epitomizes redemption and growth, from its bright and airy dining room in a former warehouse with reclaimed wood tables to the people participating in their food service training program as a means to overcome poverty. Inspiration Kitchen works with homeless and low-income Chicagoans and trains them for careers in food service, while the Inspiration Organization provides additional services to help them overcome other obstacles so they can move out of poverty.

That, however, is not the reason to visit Inspiration Kitchen. The amazing food (and fantastic prices) are what draw people in and keep them coming back. Inspiration Kitchen serves contemporary American food with some Southern style. The brunch menu includes corn meal fried green tomatoes, chicken and biscuit, and brioche French toast. For lunch and dinner, try some Nawlins' Style Gulf Crab Beignets, a pulled chicken salad, or a quinoa and veggie burger. Inspiration Kitchen also has a kids' menu. Reservations are accepted, and Inspiration Kitchen is just outside the Garfield Park Conservatory.

Entrees are between $10 and $15.
The CTA Green Line train stops at nearby Garfield Park stop.
Free parking in lot and on Lake Street.

LITTLE GOAT DINER

820 W. Randolph Street, Chicago, IL 60607
(312) 888-3455
www.littlegoatchicago.com
Open breakfast, lunch, and dinner daily.

The Little Goat Diner is a classic with a bright and shiny dining room and traditional diner favorites, but with a twist. Executive Chef Stephanie Izard—winner on the reality show competition *Top Chef* in 2008—opened this restaurant as a relaxed companion to her other restaurant, The Girl and the Goat.

As you'd expect, Little Goat serves burgers, soups, salads, "sammiches," shakes, and all-day breakfast. Surprising combinations on the menu, though, like the Fat Elvis Waffle, with peanut butter, banana, and maple syrup, or the Creole Crab Crumpets, regularly receive rave reviews, and the constant stream of customers means it's working. The kids' menu, printed on a paper placemat complete with jokes, games, and a picture to color, has pancakes, waffles, burgers and dogs, grilled cheese, mac and cheese, and chicken fingers. Little Goat is a bakery too, so grab some bagels or specialty breads to bring home.

LOU MALNATI'S

3859 W. Ogden Avenue, Chicago, IL 60623
(773) 762-0800
www.loumalnatis.com/chicago-lawndale
Open for lunch and dinner daily.

Lou Malnati's is a family-owned restaurant often nominated as a contender for the best pizza in Chicago. Since they opened in the 1940s, they've expanded to more than 45 locations throughout the Chicagoland area. When they opened 20 years ago, the Lawndale location on Ogden Avenue partnered with the Lawndale Community Church to create a job training program for Hope House, a residential program for men re-entering society after release from prison and/or recovery from substance abuse. Lou Malnati's and Lawndale have embraced each other, and 100% of the profits from this location go to helping fund educational and recreational programs for kids in the area.

As for the pizza, Lou Malnati's relies on fresh ingredients for making their pizzas and takes great pride in their buttery crust, thick vine-ripened plum tomato sauce, and exclusive sausage blend. Overall, it's like heaven in your mouth. Gluten-free pizza is also on the menu, but it's probably not quite what you'd expect—instead of using gluten-free flour, the crust is actually made with sausage! Lou Malnati's also has a kids' menu.

If you're an out-of-towner who is hooked on Lou's pizza, or you're a Chicagoan who wants to share it with distant relatives, Malnati's has you covered. They ship deep-dish pizzas anywhere in the United States.

MARIO'S ITALIAN LEMONADE

1066 W. Taylor Street, Chicago, IL 60607
Open May 1 through September from 10:00 a.m. to midnight daily.

Mario's doesn't look like much—it's just a modest wooden walk-up stand—but the lines it produces on hot summer nights say it all. Mario's opened in the 1950s and has been a city-wide favorite ever since. The Italian ice served here comes with lemon slices and other fresh fruit. Pick from a variety of seasonal flavors like pomegranate, cantaloupe, strawberry, watermelon, and piña colada, and if you order a size medium or larger, you can even request combined flavors. The lines can be long, but they move pretty fast. Mario's doesn't take credit cards, so be sure to bring cash.

Italian ice prices range from about $2 to $7. A medium will be about $3.

CTA bus route #157 stops at Taylor and Aberdeen. Routes #60 and #157 stop at Racine and Taylor a few blocks away.

Street parking is available but can be difficult to find.

WISHBONE

1001 W. Washington Boulevard, Chicago, IL 60607
(312) 850-2663
www.WishboneChicago.com
Open for breakfast and lunch on Monday and Saturday; breakfast, lunch, and dinner Tuesday through Sunday.

Walking into Wishbone you feel like you might be entering a relative's home; the staff is friendly, the seating is comfortable, and you're surrounded by colorful walls and artwork. Wishbone specializes in Southern Reconstruction cooking. They have fantastic comfort food like beef brisket, po' boys, and shrimp and grits, and a large children's menu. Tuesday night is Family Night—one free kids' entree with each adult entree purchased while vintage cartoons play on the restaurant televisions. On weekdays Wishbone offers a discount to customers who arrive by bike. Be sure you check out the artwork and the "Floop the Fly" book, all created by family members of the chef, Joel Nickson.

Entrees are about $8–$15.

The CTA Green and Pink lines stop at Morgan two blocks away. The Blue Line train stops at UIC-Halsted about half a mile away.

There is valet and street parking available.

Free Activities

- **Garfield Park Conservatory**—Experience a variety of environments and their plants, trees, and flowers.

- **Chic-A-Go-Go**—Dance your butt off during a taping of *Chic-A-Go-Go,* the cable access, all-ages dance party show, then watch yourself on cable Channel 19 Tuesdays at 8:30 p.m. and Wednesdays at 3:30 p.m.

- **Big Monster Door**—Meet a monster! You can't go in, but this is a great spot for taking some fun photos.

- **National Museum of Mexican Art**—Explore Mexican art and culture.

- **Green City Market**—Get some fresh air and fresh fruits, veggies, and flowers, or just enjoy some people-watching.

- **Juicebox**—Kid-friendly music, theater, and dance performances take place at the Garfield Park Conservatory and at the Chicago Cultural Center in the downtown area.

- **Theater Workshop at the Free Street Theater**—Get dramatic on the second Saturday of each month.

SOUTH/SOUTHWEST ✳

The South Side houses a diverse population as well as a number of so-cial and cultural institutions. The stockyards that helped Chicago become the "hog butcher of the world" were in this area, as is Midway Airport and the Kenwood and Hyde Park neighborhoods where former President Barack Obama and his family lived and worked. The city's two largest neighborhood parades—The Bud Billiken Parade and the South Side Irish Parade—are major South Side events. *The Blues Brothers* and parts of the movie *Barbershop* were filmed on the South Side of Chicago. The Orange, Red, and Green CTA train lines serve the South and Southwest side, and expressways I-55 and I-90/I-94 run through this area.

Attractions

BRONZEVILLE CHILDREN'S MUSEUM
9301 S. Stony Island Avenue, Chicago, IL 60617
(773) 721-9301
www.bronzevillechildrensmuseum.com
Open 10:00 a.m.–2:00 p.m. Tuesday through Saturday; closed Sunday and Monday

Most children's museums are open play areas where children explore on their own, but the Bronzeville Children's Museum is a little different. First of all, it is the first and only African American children's museum in the United States. Second, they use a more structured method for visitors, offering guided tours with hands-on experiences. The highly structured method they employ provides clear lessons to the children and provides messages about their own capabilities and potential.

Visitors can choose which tour they'd like to take—You Are What You Eat, African American Inventors Changing Lives, Journey to our S.T.E.M., or a tour of Bronzeville landmarks, where you can learn about becoming a banker or doctor. Tours last about 1 to 2 hours and take place hourly when the museum is open.

There are six exhibits at the Bronzeville Children's Museum: You Are What You Eat, where kids learn about the importance of healthy food; the Jewel Store to shop for healthy food; ComEd African American Inventors, which includes inventors of the light bulb and traffic light; S.T.E.M. Rocks teaches about science, technology, engineering, and math in everyday life; Illinois Service Federal Savings & Loan Association, complete with teller window and ATM; and Provident Hospital, with stethoscopes and a model of the human heart.

DR. MARTIN LUTHER KING, JR. PARK & FAMILY ENTERTAINMENT CENTER

1219 W. 76th Street, Chicago, IL 60620

(312) 747-2602

http://www.unitedskates.com/

Open 6:00 p.m.–8:30 p.m. Monday–Thursday; 4:00 p.m.–6:30 p.m. and 7:00 p.m.–10:00 p.m. Friday; noon–3:00 p.m., 3:30 p.m.–6:30 p.m., and 7:00 p.m.–10:00 p.m. Saturday; 3:00 p.m.–7:30 p.m. Sunday. Schedule may vary during school breaks or holidays.

Although many of the classic Chicago roller rinks are no longer around, the Dr. Martin Luther King, Jr. Park & Family Entertainment Center, which opened in 2003, still offers roller skating, bowling, and an arcade, as well as concessions. The bowling alley has 12 lanes and the roller rink can hold 500 skaters, so bring your friends! Public skating and bowling are offered daily, and skating lessons are available on Saturday mornings for $5, including skate rental. Skate Mate Trainers are available for rent, too. Rollerbladers are welcome.

Special events are scheduled regularly, including Home School Skate, 21-and-over skate nights, holiday celebrations, specials during school breaks, and summer skate camp. They also offer a number of group packages, birthday party options, and school fundraisers.

DUSABLE MUSEUM OF AFRICAN AMERICAN HISTORY

740 E. 56th Place, Chicago, IL 60637
(773) 947-0600
http://www.dusablemuseum.org
Open Tuesday–Saturday 10:00 a.m.–5:00 p.m., Sunday noon–5:00 p.m. Closed
Monday. Closed most major holidays.

Founded in the 1960s, the DuSable Museum in Hyde Park was the first
museum of its kind in the country, and it remains one of the few independent
institutions of its kind. The museum holds more than 15,000 pieces, including
paintings, historical memorabilia, and sculptures, to help preserve and interpret
the experiences and achievements of people of African descent. Visitors can
learn about Harold Washington, Chicago's first African American mayor; the history of Blacks in the Armed Services; and the Journey to Equality. In addition to
its permanent exhibits, the museum also hosts special exhibitions, lectures, and
workshops, and an annual MLK Day Family Celebration. The DuSable Museum is
small, but the space has been expanded to include a roundhouse expected to be
completed sometime in 2017.

Insider tip: Parents, teachers, and students can also access free educational
information and works of art digitally through the DuSable Museum website.

$10/adult, $3/child ages 6–11, children 5 and under free. Chicago residents:
$8/adult, $2/child.

Admission is free on Sundays.

Best for ages 5 and up.

Time to explore: 1–2 hours

The CTA Red and Green lines and several bus routes are nearby.

Free parking in lot.

MIDWAY PLAISANCE PARK ICE RINK

1130 Midway Plaisance, Chicago, IL 60637
(312) 745-2470
www.chicagoparkdistrict.com/parks/Midway-Plaisance
Open 12:00 a.m.–7:00 p.m. Monday through Friday, 2:00 p.m.–9:00 p.m. on
Saturday, 1:00 p.m.–6:00 p.m. on Sunday.

More than a century ago it was the site of the world's first Ferris wheel at the
1893 World's Columbian Exposition; today, the spins at Midway Plaisance are on
a much smaller scale. Lace up those skates and glide (or lurch and teeter) onto
the ice of this outdoor rink and create some warm winter memories. Sure, Millennium Park offers ice skating too, but at Midway Plaisance you get many of the
benefits—a beautiful view, a warming center, low prices—without the crowds.
Bring a sled too! There's plenty space in the park for little ones to do some
sledding.

On Saturday mornings, they offer skate lessons for only $10, and rat hockey pick-up games are available on Monday and Wednesday evenings or on Saturday and Sunday for only $10. The Chicago Blackhawks sometimes host free clinics here too (registration required).

In the summer the Chicago Park District hosts movies and concerts here, and it's also the location for the Hyde Park Jazz Fest.

Insider tip: Visit on Family Night (Saturdays from 5:30 p.m. to 9:00 p.m.) when a family of five skates for only $10, including skate rentals.

$5 admission for adults; $4 for adult skate rental. Children with skates are free; rental skates for children are $6.

Best for ages 5 and up.

Time to explore: 1–3 hours (or as long as you can handle the cold!)

CTA bus routes #2, #171, and #172 stop at 60th and Kenwood, and #171, #172, and #192 stop at 59th and Kimbark. The Metra ME train line stops at the 59th Street (University of Chicago) station nearby.

Free street parking is available.

MT. GREENWOOD PARK PLAYGROUND

3721 W. 111th Street, Chicago, IL 60655
(312) 747-6561
http://www.chicagoparkdistrict.com/parks/Mt-Greenwood-Park
Open 6:00 a.m.–11:00 p.m. daily.

The playground is one of those things kids and parents both love—kids get to explore, climb, and meet new friends while parents get to sit for a bit and maybe even have a conversation with another adult. Mt. Greenwood Park will exceed expectations for both children and their parents. The unique design, with rubbery hills, a variety of classic and modern play structures and rides, musical components, swings, and a splash pad, will excite children and keep them busy and active for a long time. Meanwhile, parents can relax on benches or at tables, in the sun or the shade, and they don't have to worry about their kids getting away—the entire playground is enclosed by a fence with only a single gate for entry and exit. There's free parking in the attached lot and a fieldhouse with bathrooms just on the other side of the lot.

Insider tip: Don't forget swimsuits and a towel (or a change of clothes) in the summer for the splash pad.

Free

Best for ages 8 and younger.

Time to explore: 1–3 hours

CTA bus route #112 stops at 111th Street and Hamlin.

Free parking in attached lot.

MUSEUM OF SCIENCE AND INDUSTRY

5700 S. Lake Shore Drive, Chicago, IL 60637
(773) 684-1414
www.msichicago.org
Open 9:30 a.m.–4:00 p.m. most days; see website for select days when the MSI
stays open until 5:30 p.m.

Visit the Museum of Science and Industry to explore a real plane, train, and
submarine. Learn about the science of storms, examine the giant miniature
fairy castle, and learn all about YOU! in an exhibit that explores the connection between the mind, the body, and the spirit. You can travel inside a U-505
German submarine and an underground coal mine, see The Great Train Story (a
model train display featuring Chicago and Seattle), watch chicks hatch, and step
inside a 40-foot tornado. The Museum of Science and Industry has more than 20
permanent exhibits, and many rotating exhibits as well, and a staggering number
of transportation objects—a 1903 Wright Flyer replica, Boeing 727, 999 Steam
Locomotive, "Jenny" biplane, the *Pioneer Zephyr*, and WWII Stuka dive-bomber
are just some of the vehicles on display.

Young scientists under the age of 10 will love the Idea Factory, a play and
experimentation area where they can get wet at the water table while they learn
about floating objects, test weight distributions by lifting things with a toy crane,
and use air tubes to discover the power of air pressure. The Idea Factory also has
a family bathroom and a comfortable nursing room.

The Museum of Science and Industry hosts Christmas Around the World and
Holiday Lights during the holiday season. This event is included in the general
admission fee.

Insider tip: There are a lot of activities not included in the general admission,
but you can choose to be thrifty and still have plenty to do to fill a day at the
museum. Spring for extra activities if you want, but they're definitely not a
necessity. There is easily enough here to fill a couple days' worth of visits. If you
have time to visit again, consider purchasing an annual pass.

General admission is $18 for adults, $11 for children ages 3–11 years old.
The Omnimax shows, FabLab, U-505 Sub Tour, Coal Mine, and Future Energy
Chicago cost extra.

Best for children ages 3 and up.

Time to explore: 3–6 hours

Metra Electric Line and South Shore Line trains stop at the 55th/56th/57th Street
station two blocks away. CTA bus route #2 Hyde Park Express stops at 57th and
Stony Island; route #6 Jackson Park Express stops at 56th Street and Hyde Park.

Parking in the underground garage at the museum is $22.

ORIENTAL INSTITUTE

1155 E. 158th Street, Chicago, IL 60637
(773) 702-9514
http://www.oi.uchicago.edu
Open Tuesday, Thursday–Sunday 10:00 a.m.–5:00 p.m., Wednesday 10:00
a.m.–8:00 p.m. Closed Mondays.

The Oriental Institute is dedicated to research and study of the ancient Near
East. They are a world-renowned institute for history, art, and archeology, and
they showcase objects found during excavations and displayed in exhibits devoted to ancient Egypt, Nubia, Persia, Mesopotamia, Syria, Anatolia, and Megiddo.
Stop by to see the colossal 17-foot-tall statue of King Tutankhamun and try to
decipher the ancient hieroglyphs. The Oriental Institute offers a homeschool
workshop, Junior Archeologists events, and other family-friendly programs,
generally intended for children ages 5–12 years old. They also occasionally host
stroller tours for parents with infants or toddlers.

Insider tip: This is a great place to visit
on the weekends. It's not too busy, and
because it's on a college campus it's much
easier to park on evenings and weekends
than during the week.

Free admission. Suggested donation of
$10/adult, $5/child under age 12.

Best for ages 5 and up.

Time to explore: 2–3 hours

Garfield Boulevard bus stops at University
Avenue, three blocks from the Oriental
Institute.

Street parking is difficult; parking garage at
55th and Ellis costs $8–$25. Free parking
after 4:00 p.m. and all day on weekends at
Lexington parking lot half a block south of
the museum.

PROMONTORY POINT AT BURNHAM PARK

5491 S. Shore Drive, Chicago, IL 60615
(312) 742-5369
http://www.chicagoparkdistrict.com/parks/BurnhamPark
Open 6:00 a.m.–11:00 p.m. daily.

Just south of Grant Park is Burnham Park, a quiet, 600-acre green space on the
Lake Michigan shore where you're unlikely to find crowds. Promontory Point is
a man-made peninsula that juts out into Lake Michigan, providing exceptional
views of the Chicago landscape. Stones are built up along the shoreline to create
large stone steps. Kids will love climbing around and playing on the rocks, and
there's plenty of room for picnicking. Public bathrooms are available here.

Promontory Point is blocks away from Printer's Row—where you can find a variety of restaurants—and less than a mile from the Museum of Science and Industry. Burnham Park also has a beach, and a skate park is nearby.

Insider tip: Don't plan to swim here. You can, but it's mostly rock without much sand and definitely not a good place for swimming with kids.

Free

Good for all ages.

Time to explore: 1–2 hours

CTA bus route #171 stops at Shoreland Dorm.

Metered parking in nearby lots.

PULLMAN NATIONAL MONUMENT
11141 S. Cottage Grove, Chicago, IL 60628
(773) 785-8901
http://www.pullmanil.org
Open Tuesday–Sunday 11:00 a.m.–3:00 p.m. Closed Mondays.

The historic Pullman area was built in the 1880s as a company town providing housing and other needs for employees of the Pullman Car Company and was the site of the famous Pullman strike. Now it's a Chicago landmark and was dedicated as a national monument by President Barack Obama in February 2015.

Start out your visit at the Visitor Center to see photos, artifacts, and a short introductory film. You can pick up a map and brochure to take your own tour of the area, or visit on the first Sunday of the month between May and October for a guided tour. Make no mistake—Pullman isn't a museum, but a living, breathing neighborhood, with a number of historic homes and sites. There is an Annual House Tour in October (dates vary each year) when visitors can see inside private homes.

Fun fact: Pullman was featured in the movies *Road to Perdition, The Fugitive, The Express,* and was the inspiration for the animated scenes at the North Pole in *The Polar Express.*

Insider tip: Kids can get a Jr. Ranger Explorer sheet and a Jr. Ranger badge sticker at the Visitor Center.

Free admission to the Visitor Center. Guided tours are $10 for adults and $7 for students.

Best for grade schoolers and older kids.

Time to explore: 1–2 hours

Take CTA bus route #111 Pullman to Cottage Grove and 112th Street.

Free parking in lot.

SMART MUSEUM OF ART

The University of Chicago, 5550 S. Greenwood Avenue, Chicago, IL 60637
(773) 702-0200
http://www.smartmuseum.uchicago.edu
Closed Monday. Tuesday–Wednesday and Friday–Sunday 10:00 a.m.–5:00 p.m.,
Thursday 10:00 a.m.–8:00 p.m.

Whether you're looking for something small enough to explore thoroughly in a few hours or just wanting to see something new, the Smart Museum of Art is a great place to bring the family. This is the fine arts museum of the University of Chicago and although it's small, it offers bold artwork in both permanent and rotating exhibits. There are over 15,000 pieces here, with Modern, Asian, European, and Contemporary art represented. The Smart Museum has an outdoor sculpture garden as well. There's a café in the museum, with outdoor seating when weather permits.

The Smart Museum has Family Day one Saturday a month; there's a different theme each month, with coordinating activities and art projects. Admission for these events is free, and they are geared toward kids between 4 and 12 years old.

Insider tip: Stop by the front desk for a family guide.

Free

Best for ages 4 and up.

Time to explore: 1–2 hours

#55 Garfield bus, #2 Hyde Park Express, and #4 Cottage Grove bus are all within walking distance.

Weekday parking is difficult; free parking is available on weekends and evenings one block away on University Campus North parking garage.

Sports

WHITE SOX

Guaranteed Rate Stadium (previously U.S. Cellular Field and Comiskey Park), 333 W. 35th Street, Chicago, IL 60616
(866) 800-1275
http://www.whitesox.com
Season runs from April to October.

Chicagoans have an undying loyalty to their city and to their baseball team, but for some that baseball team is the Cubs, and for others it's the Sox. Although there are other cities that also have two teams, the crosstown rivalry in Chicago has gone on the longest, stretching back more than a century. The South Siders (from primarily blue-collar neighborhoods) and the North Siders (from more middle- and upper-class neighborhoods) may never see entirely eye-to-eye, but everyone enjoys the annual battle over the Crosstown Cup when the two teams play each other.

The Chicago White Sox began playing in Chicago in 1900, with a string of famous players throughout the years including Paul Konerko, Frank Thomas, and Carlton Fisk, and their most recent World Series Championship came in 2005. The White Sox encourage families to attend games with family-friendly events and activities. Fireworks kick off every game, and they'll also go off every time the White Sox get a home run and after a White Sox victory. There are activities for kids during the game at the Xfinity Fundamentals area, where there are clinics, practice, and skills instruction. Speed pitch machines are also available during games. Also, if you're visiting with a small child or children, stop at the Guest Relations Booth to get them a wristband personalized with their seat number so employees can bring them back to their seats if they get lost.

Pint-sized fans can join the White Sox kids club. Sign them up for a free Slugger membership and they'll receive temporary tattoos, a wall cling, and two upper reserved tickets. If you choose the $30 Allstar membership, they'll receive plenty of White Sox gear, invitations to special events, four Lower Level Outfield reserved tickets, and additional perks.

Side note: The White Sox used to play at Comiskey Park, but in 2003 the name was changed to U.S. Cellular Field. Fans couldn't get used to the name change, continuing to refer to it as Comiskey Park, or "Comiskullar." In 2016 the name was changed again, and it's now Guaranteed Rate Field. It's unlikely that fans will accept this name, but the contract is scheduled to remain in place until 2029.

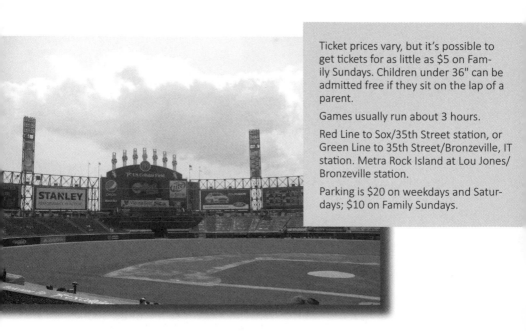

Ticket prices vary, but it's possible to get tickets for as little as $5 on Family Sundays. Children under 36" can be admitted free if they sit on the lap of a parent.

Games usually run about 3 hours.

Red Line to Sox/35th Street station, or Green Line to 35th Street/Bronzeville, IT station. Metra Rock Island at Lou Jones/Bronzeville station.

Parking is $20 on weekdays and Saturdays; $10 on Family Sundays.

Restaurants

CONNIE'S PIZZA

2373 S. Archer Avenue, Chicago, IL 60616
(312) CONNIES
http://www.conniespizza.com/archer-avenue
Open Sunday–Monday 11:00 a.m.–10:00 p.m., Tuesday–Thursday 11:00 a.m.–
11:00 p.m., Friday and Saturday 11:00 a.m.–midnight.

Connie's has several locations throughout the city and suburbs, but this one in the Bridgeport neighborhood of Chicago is their flagship location. The high-ceiling brick warehouse is adorned with black-and-white photos, vintage advertisements, old gears and machinery, barrels, and plenty of tomato cans, and it's very charming. Connie's is a pretty popular place, especially on weekends, but the huge building usually manages the crowds pretty well.

Pan pizza is Connie's specialty, but they also offer deep dish, stuffed, and thin crust. There are a number of Italian and American food choices on the menu if you're not in the mood for pizza. There's a kids' menu, including an option to build their own pizza. A drink, meal, and dessert for children is about $6, and kids get to take home their cup.

Connie's pizza is the official pizza of the Chicago Blackhawks and the Chicago Bulls, so you'll find it served at all their games. They also offer carry-out, delivery, and catering. There are coupons and specials listed on their website, and you can join their loyalty club for special perks.

During baseball season, Connie's offers a free shuttle to and from the game for fans who eat at Connie's beforehand.

Entrees are about $10–$15; a large original pan pizza is about $20.

CTA bus routes #44 and #62 stop at Archer and Grove.

Free parking in lot.

EMPEROR'S CHOICE RESTAURANT

2238 S. Wentworth Avenue, Chicago, IL 60616
(312) 225-8800
http://emporerschoicerestaurant.com
Open 11:30 a.m.–10:00 p.m. daily.

Emperor's Choice Restaurant doesn't stand out much from the other buildings on Wentworth Avenue in Chinatown until you take a closer look at the beautifully detailed pillars and balcony.

Emperor's Choice serves Cantonese and Szechwan dishes, including Mongolian beef, fried rice, moo shu pork, and Dungeness crab. They have lunch specials and offer a variety of vegetarian choices. There's no kids' menu, but you can order a few dishes to share among those at the table.

Carry out and delivery are also available. The owner also has restaurants with similar menus in other locations—Mo's 1 and Mo's 2, both in Orland Park, and Mo's Asian Bistro near Fullerton and Southport.

Insider tip: Chinatown Square is just a couple blocks away, where you can view 12 Chinese zodiac sculptures, a mural, and two pagodas with stairs.

Dishes range from about $10 to $35.

CTA bus route #24 stops at Wentworth and 24th Street; bus route #21 and the Red Line train stop at the Cermak-Chinatown station.

Street parking is available but can be difficult to find.

NANA

3267 S. Halsted Street, Chicago, IL 60608
(312) 929-2486
www.nanaorganic.com
Open for breakfast and lunch Monday and Tuesday, and breakfast, lunch, and dinner Wednesday through Sunday.

Nana serves American food with Latin flair and specializes in local, sustainable, and organic food. The dining room has exposed brick, wood floors and tables, hanging lights, and white walls; it's chic and comfortable. Kids have choices like the teddy bear pancake or mini waffles for breakfast, but lunch and dinner are also available all day and come with homemade apple sauce. Mom and Dad can choose from an extensive menu, including hot cocoa pancakes, empanadas, or ancho chile braised short ribs.

There's a transparency in Nana's food preparation you don't find many places; not only is the food prepared in an open kitchen, but you can even find out about all their local farmers and producers on their website. If you become a regular customer at Nana, you need to check out their rewards program, in which you get $15 back for every $250 you spend there. Visit on Wednesday, Thursday, or Friday night between 5 and 7 p.m. for their "kids eat free" promotion.

Kids' menu items are available for about $5–$6; entrees prices range from about $13 to $30.

The Red Line train stops at Sox-35th Street, one mile away.

Street parking is easy to find.

THE ORIGINAL RAINBOW CONE

9233 S. Western Avenue, Chicago, IL 60643
(773) 238-7075
http://www.rainbowcone.com
Open seasonally, noon–9:00 p.m.

There are some copycats, but no one does the ice cream rainbow like The Original Rainbow Cone, where they've been serving them for nine decades. This south-side favorite is made up of five ice cream flavors stacked on an angle (from bottom to top): chocolate, strawberry, Palmer House (New York vanilla with cherries and walnuts), pistachio, and orange sherbet. Rainbow Cone has a variety of other flavors, but why would you want them when you can have a rainbow cone? As with most really good ice cream places, there are long lines on hot days, but they've streamlined their process to shorten the wait. Baby cones are available for little ones; the name is a bit misleading, because there is plenty of ice cream in these!

Cones are less than $5.

CTA bus route #95 stops at Western and 92nd Place.

Free parking in lot.

Free Activities

- **Promontory Point**—Get an amazing view of the skyline at Promontory Point in Burnham Park.

- **Tour Obama's neighborhood**—President Barack Obama spent many years living in Chicago and has adopted Chicago as his hometown. See where it all began with this guide to Obama's neighborhood and other nearby places of significance to the first family: http://www.alltrails.com/trail/us/illinois/hyde-park-kenwood-and-south-shore-neighborhoods-walking-tour?referrer=everytrail.

- **Oriental Institute Museum**—Learn about Near Eastern civilizations. Check their calendar for family programs and workshops.

- **Palmisano Park**—Walk, hike, fish, or just take in the view at one of the city's most interesting green spaces in Chicago, located in the Bridgeport neighborhood.

- **Jackson Park**—This Woodlawn park has Japanese-style Osaka Garden and other fun features.

✳ NORTH SUBURBS ✳

The north suburbs area of Chicago is an affluent area, home to many white-collar families. The variety of family-friendly places here is great, and there are some lovely public spaces as well. I-90, I-94, and I-294 run through the area, and although the public transportation isn't as plentiful as in the city, parking is usually easy to find.

Attractions

ACTORS GYMNASIUM
Noyes Cultural Arts Center, 927 Noyes Street, Evanston, IL 60201
(847) 328-2795
www.actorsgymnasium.org
Open 10:00 a.m.–5:30 p.m. Monday through Friday, 10:00 a.m.–noon Saturday; closed Sunday.

It's a bird! It's a plane! It's your son or daughter swinging on a trapeze! Get your kids off the couch and into the air, or onto a unicycle, or twirling in silks. The Actors Gymnasium is a non-profit organization for circus arts, physical theatre, and multi-disciplinary performance. Kids as young as 2 years old can take classes in the parent-tot circus. Older kids can choose from a variety of workshops, enroll in weekly camp sessions, or join the Youth Circus. Acrodance, aerial arts, stilts, parkour, tight-wire, juggling, clowning, and contortion are just some of the amazing skills they can learn. Actors Gymnasium also offers special needs classes. Students can perform in circus shows for family and friends.

Insider tip: Tallmadge Park is just next door and is a nice distraction for children when a sibling is taking a class.

$20 tickets for circus shows; cost of classes and camps vary.

Classes available for ages 2 and up.

Shows are about 90 minutes. The duration of classes varies.

CTA Purple Line trains stop at the Noyes station.

There is a small parking lot with metered parking. Drop-offs are recommended when possible.

ARLINGTON INTERNATIONAL RACECOURSE

2200 W. Euclid Avenue, Arlington Heights, IL 60005
(847) 385-7500
http://www.arlingtonpark.com
Racing seasonally from May through September. There are some special events October through April. Open Friday–Sunday and some Thursdays.

You've probably seen it in a movie or two—the irresponsible uncle or grand-father takes a child to "the track." What are they thinking?? Surprisingly, it's not such a bad idea after all. Visiting Arlington Racecourse can be an activity for the whole family, especially on Family Day. Of course, no one under 21 can bet, but it's still fun to cheer on your favorite horse. Besides the fresh air and the excite-ment of the racing, there are inflatables, face painting, and a petting zoo on Family Day. You can bring in outside food and drinks, but they are allowed only in the park and reserved canopy tables on the Apron Level.

Insider tip: Don't forget sun protection. There is very little shade available outside unless you purchase pricey seats.

General admission is $6–$8 for adults, $4 for children. Premium events are $16, and fireworks nights are $20.

Reserved seating is $8–$32, and reserved tables are $18–$55.

Good for all ages.

Time to explore: There are several races, lasting a total of about 5 hours.

The Metra UP-NW train stops at the Arlington Park station.

Free parking in lot.

BOWEN PARK

1800 N. Sheridan Road, Waukegan, IL 60085
(847) 360-4725
http://www.waukeganparks.org/location/bowen-park
Open 7:15 a.m. to 8:45 p.m. daily

All parks are not created equal, and Bowen Park in Waukegan is proof of that. The playground is positioned on a hill with rubber-surfaced moguls and wooden steps to reach the top. Giant play structures with bridges and rope ladders have 40-foot-long slides that take kids all the way to the bottom of the hill. There are swings, a spinning ride, and a separate area for toddlers. At the bottom of the hill is a splash pad as well as the highlight of the park—an enormous spider web. The spider web has a spiral shape so it's easy enough to walk to the top, but there are plenty of ways to climb and hang if your kid is a natural climber. There are safety nets inside the web so parents can breathe a little easier even when the kids are way up high.

With 61 acres, there's plenty of green space surrounding the playground, so pack a picnic lunch and make it a day. A pavilion, restrooms, and plenty of bench-es and picnic tables make it a comfortable place to visit for hours.

Insider tip: Wear comfortable clothes and shoes in case you have to rescue a little one from the top of the web.

Free

Best for ages 2 and up.

Time to explore: 2–4 hours

Pace bus route #571 stops at Sheridan and Greenwood.

Plenty of free parking in attached parking lot.

DAD'S SLOT CARS

700 Lee Street, Des Plaines, IL 60016
(847) 298-0688
www.dadsslotcars.com
Open noon–8:30 p.m. Tuesday through Saturday, noon–5:00 p.m. Sunday. Closed Monday.

Sometimes the best way to do something new is to return to something old, so chuck the video game controller and switch to a three-dimensional game—slot car racing. Dad's has been family owned and operated since 1992, and they rent and sell 1/24 and 1/32 scale model race cars. Track time is available by the half hour, and Dad's will provide the track, car, and controller. Will you slow down a bit at the turns, or hit the throttle and watch the cars crash, and fly off the track?

Enjoy a couple of scoops or a soda in the small ice cream shop in the back of the store. You can also book a party. Be sure to bring cash, because credit cards are not accepted.

Insider tip: Dad's offers free track time for each "A" on a report card, so cash in on those good grades!

Cost is $10 for half an hour of track time, rental of a car, and rental of a controller.

Best for grade schoolers and up.

1–2 hours

Pace bus routes #226, #230, and #250 stop at Lee/Ellinwood; the Metra UP-NW train Des Plaines stop is nearby.

Street parking is available.

CHICAGO BOTANIC GARDENS

1000 Lake Cook Road, Glencoe, IL 60022
(847) 835-5440
http://www.chicagobotanic.org
Open 8:00 a.m.–7:00 p.m. daily.

Many museums display remnants of the past, but the Chicago Botanic Gardens is a museum of living plants. With 26 different gardens on over 300 acres, you can see everything from an English walled garden to a Japanese garden to a fruit and vegetable garden. Kids will probably enjoy the Sensory Garden, where visitors are invited to see, smell, and even touch the plants; plants are in raised beds to make them accessible to those in wheelchairs (or strollers). The Enabling Garden is another great area to visit; this hands-on teaching garden is designed for people of all ages and abilities. Don't miss the Children's Growing Garden, where kids can water, weed, and harvest plants, and on weekends they have additional drop-in activities.

The Chicago Botanic Gardens has a Model Railroad Garden that's open from May to October annually. There's a fee ($6 for adults, $4 for children ages 3–12), but it's really worth checking out. There are 18 garden-scale trains, scenes made from natural materials, like sticks, bark, pebbles, and acorns, and nearly 50 mini landmarks including the Hollywood sign, the White House, and Wrigley Field. Butterflies and Blooms is another summer exhibit with a fee, where you can enter the habitat of hundreds of butterflies.

The Chicago Botanic Gardens has trains for the holidays too—the Wonderland Express runs in November and December. The Wonderland Express is an indoor railroad garden complete with miniature Chicago landmarks and indoor snow! Tickets must be purchased for this event.

There's a café in the Visitor's Center, and tram rides are available for a fee.

Insider tip: Wear comfortable shoes and bring some bottles of water, because there's a lot of walking to do here!

Admission is free; you pay only for parking.

Good for all ages.

Time to explore: 3–6 hours

The Metra UP-N Line train stops at Braeside Metra Station almost a mile away. Pace bus route #213/"Northbrook Court" stops at the Chicago Botanic Garden. There is also a trolley that runs from the Glencoe Metra Station on Sundays May through September.

Parking is $25/car on weekdays, $30 on weekends. Vans are $30 each.

EXPLORITORIUM

4701 Oakton Street, Skokie, IL 60076
(847) 674-1500
http://www.skokieparks.org/exploritorium
Open Monday–Wednesday and Friday 9:00 a.m.–5:00 p.m., Saturday
9:00 a.m.–1:00 p.m. Closed Thursday and Sunday.

It's hard to decide whether the Exploritorium is a very small children's museum or a large indoor play café, but what's really important is that it's a ton of fun. The Exploritorium is part of the Skokie Park District, and it's truly a treasure. The play area has a half-wall with a door at the entrance so little kids can't leave without a parent. The play area has different sections, but it's all very open, allowing parents to observe all their kids even if they're not engaged in the same activities. A giant Lite Brite wall, paint and water walls, a dress-up stage, a transportation station, and the engineering megastation are likely to keep kids busy for a long time, but there's also a large water table, a climbing wall, and a giant play structure with lots of ropes to climb, tunnels to explore, and slides to zoom down. Little ones have their very own toddler zone with age-appropriate toys and displays. On the other side of the wall is an area with a vending machine and a few tables so you can stop for a snack or bring your own lunch.

Insider tip: This is a great place to meet up for a playdate. There's plenty for kids to do, accommodations for a lunch or snack, and it's easy to keep an eye on the kids.

$3 for residents, $5 for non-residents. Children under 1 are free.

Best for ages 1 to 8.

Time to explore: 2–3 hours

Bus route #97 stops at Oakton and Knox.

Free parking in lot.

FUNTOPIA

2050 Tower Drive, Glenview, IL 60026
(224) 432-5435
www.funtopiaworld.com/glenview
Open 10:00 a.m.–8:00 p.m. Sunday through Thursday, 10:00 a.m.–9:00 p.m.
Friday and Saturday.

The name Funtopia makes quite a promise, but it does not disappoint. Imagine all the things your child does that make you gasp with fear—balancing on an unsteady pile of blocks or toys, climbing to the highest point in the park, jumping from anything they can climb onto. Now add a harness and belaying system (and a deep sigh of relief). That's Funtopia.

Funtopia has 50 climbing elements and activities, including colorful fun walls with interactive challenges, a free fall zone, a rope course, trampolines, and a drop slide. Before kids climb they watch a training video with safety rules, then they are hooked up to a harness with a belaying system to catch them if they fall. Don't tell the kids, but it's not all just fun and games either. Many of the activities here, like the rope courses, trampolines, and climbing walls, help kids work on flexibility, balance, and strength.

Kids who are too young or too cautious for the daredevil stunts won't miss out on fun either, because there's a soft play area with obstacles, a maze, and a ball jam room. There's also a cave for kids to explore, complete with miner's helmets. Funtopia has a café if climbing makes the kids hungry and they offer birthday party packages.

Different activities at Funtopia have different age, weight, or height requirements, so it's a good idea to check the website or call before you go, and make sure you know your child's current weight and measurements so they aren't turned away when you arrive.

Insider tip: Make a reservation online and prepay to ensure your child's spot.

Jungle gym admission is $10. FunWalls admission is $14 for 1 hour, $21 for 2 hours. Cave, Freefall, Drop Slide, and Ropes Course all require additional fees.

Best for ages 1 and up.

Time to explore: 1–2 hours

Pace bus route #423 stops at Patriot Boulevard.

Free parking in lot.

HELLER NATURE CENTER

2821 Ridge Road, Highland Park, IL 60035
(847) 433-6901
http://www.pdhp.org/heller-nature-center
Open Monday–Friday 8:30 a.m.–5:00 p.m., Saturday 9:00 a.m.–3:00 p.m. Closed Sunday.

Heller Nature Center is on a 97-acre preserve with three miles of trails. The nature center offers nature exhibits and an abundance of programs and special events—campfires, astronomy, beekeeping—and much more. It's a beautiful spot to picnic, and you can even sign up for canoeing adventures. Younger kids can spend some time in Wander Woods Natural Play Space, a simple wooded play area with basic tools like wheelbarrows and shovels, as well as water, mud, and sticks for natural play. Feeling adventurous? Rent some cross-country skis and explore the preserve.

Insider tip: Turn your nature walk into a treasure hunt by doing some letterboxing. Haven't heard of it? Learn more at www.letterboxing.org and get the clues you need to find the hidden letterbox at Heller Nature Center.

KOHL CHILDREN'S MUSEUM
2100 Patriot Boulevard, Glenview, IL 60026
(847) 832-6600
http://www.kohlchildrensmuseum.org
Open Monday 9:30 a.m.–noon, Tuesday–Saturday 9:30 a.m.–5:00 p.m., Sunday
noon–5:00 p.m.

All children love to imagine what they'll be when they grow up, and they can
test out the possibilities at the Kohl Children's Museum. X-ray a (stuffed) snake at
the veterinarian's office, feed and rock a baby in the nursery, be the mechanic at
the car center, paint and carpet a house, serve sandwiches at the play café, and
then work or shop at the local Whole Foods. There are 17 permanent exhibits
here, and they often have a temporary exhibit created by the staff at Kohl that
will then travel to other museums around the country, or they have one created
by another museum. Kohl has lots of conveniences parents will appreciate, like
hand dryers outside the Water Works room, family bathrooms, areas for feeding
babies, and small soft play areas for babies and toddlers next to exhibits for older
kids.

You can grab lunch at the Cosi Café at the entrance to the museum, visit a
restaurant within walking distance at The Glen Town Center, or bring your own
food—there are tables outside the museum.

Insider tip: The grocery store is a favorite exhibit for
most kids. To prevent overcrowding, the museum
puts a cap on the number of kids in the exhibit at
a time, so keep an eye on it and make your move
when the line is short.

$12 per person. Children under 1 are free.

Recommended for children from birth to age 8.

Time to explore: 3–5 hours

Metra Milwaukee District North Line at North Glenview Station is half a mile from the museum.

There is free parking in the attached lot. On busy
days when the lot is full, there is free parking in the
nearby parking garage for The Glen Town Center.

LAMBS FARM PETTING ZOO

14245 W. Rockland Road, Libertyville, IL 60048
(847) 362-4636
http://www.lambsfarm.org
Open seasonally; closes in late October. Open 10:00 a.m.–4:00 p.m. weekdays,
10:00 a.m.–5:00 p.m. weekends. On Mondays only, the farmyard is open, but no
attractions.

Lambs Farm is a non-profit organization that provides vocational and residential services to 250+ adults with developmental disabilities. They have a variety of businesses, including a petting zoo open during the warmer months. Kids can get up close to farmyard animals like cattle, horses, sheep, goats, llamas, potbelly pigs, and rabbits. There's also a mini train ride, carousel, mini golf, and a bounce house. While you're there, stop by and visit some of the other Lambs Farm businesses: Magnolia Café & Bakery, Sugar Maple Country Store, Dogwood Garden & Pet Center, and Cedar Chest Thrift Shop. Although the Petting Zoo is closed during colder months, Lambs Farm still has events and activities open to the public (for a fee) for holidays like Christmas and Valentine's Day.

Insider tip: Farmyards equal bugs, so mosquito repellent isn't a bad idea.

Admission to farmyard is $5 for children from age 2 to adults. Rides are an additional fee, or you can purchase a day pass for $12 for children ages 2–12, $8 for adults.

Best for ages 8 and younger.

Time to explore: 1–2 hours

There is no public transportation nearby.

Free parking in lot.

LITTLE BEANS

430 Asbury Avenue, Evanston, IL 60202
(847) 807-3731
http://www.littlebeanscafe.com/evanston
Open Monday–Friday 8:30 a.m.–7:00 p.m., Saturday 8:30 a.m.–3:00 p.m.,
Sunday 8:30 a.m.–3:00 p.m.

After success with their first location on the north side of Chicago, Little Beans opened a new location in Evanston recently and turned the idea of an indoor play area on its head. As you would expect, there is a play area for "little beans" (children 0–6) with a mini town square, ride-on toys, trains, LEGOs, and a seating area for parents. However, "big beans" (kids 5–12) can have some active fun too in the custom Ninja Warrior obstacle course, which includes a foam pit and zip line. There's also a dress-up area and karaoke, an EyePlay interactive floor system, and a variety of games. With a half-court gym and classrooms, Little Beans also offers drop-in sports and activities, classes for kids and adults, and it's a great place to host a birthday party or other event.

Little Beans has a café with coffee, pastries, breakfast, lunch, and a kids' menu. Non-holiday Mondays are half price, and memberships are available. Remember to bring your socks or you can purchase a pair at the café.

MARRIOTT THEATRE—THEATRE FOR YOUNG AUDIENCES

10 Marriott Drive, Lincolnshire, IL 60069
(847) 634-0200
http://www.marriotttheatre.com/childrens-theatre
Schedules vary. Children's shows are generally at 10:00 am or 12:30 p.m. Tuesday through Saturday.

The Marriott Theatre in Lincolnshire has a variety of mainstage shows, and children under the age of 6 are not admitted, but they also have Theatre for Young Audiences created especially for children and performed during the morning or early afternoon. With an arena stage and only about eight rows of seats, there's not a bad seat in the house. Shows are about an hour long with no intermission and are usually followed by a question and answer session with the cast. Past shows have included *The Nutcracker, Seussical, Wizard of Oz, Schoolhouse Rock,* and *Madagascar—A Musical Adventure.* There's no dress code here— you'll see audience members wearing everything from jeans to dress clothes, with lots of kids dressed up in fancy theater dresses or suits.

The Theatre is part of the Marriott Lincolnshire Resort, so if you're coming from out of town (or just want to plan a special getaway) you can book overnight accommodations. The resort also has several dining options if you'd like to have lunch or dinner after the show.

100

RAVINIA FESTIVAL

418 Sheridan Road, Highland Park, IL 60035
(847) 266-5100
www.Ravinia.org
Ravinia is open seasonally. Show times vary.

Ravinia is the oldest outdoor music festival in the United States. This concert venue hosts everything from musicians, to circus performances, to ballet, and has hosted performances from Yo-Yo Ma, the Beach Boys, Billie Corgan, and many more. During each three-month-long season, Ravinia hosts approximately 120–150 performances and events, so there's definitely something for everyone.

The pavilion seats 3,400 and provides a more traditional concert experience, but the real fun is in the lawn section. Food is available for purchase, but most people choose to bring their own, some even setting up elaborate picnics. You can rent tables and chairs or bring your own blanket and chairs. You can't really see the stage, but you can hear it, and for some concerts there are screens so you don't miss what's happening on the stage. KidsLawn Interactive Musical Playground is on the north lawn area during select children's shows, and kids can do arts and crafts, check out a "petting zoo of instruments," and make their own music with large-scale percussion instruments.

Insider tip: Arrive early so you can stake out a good spot.

Ticket prices vary a great deal, but for children's concerts, lawn seats are only $5 per person. Children under 15 years old are admitted to the lawn for free for classical shows.

Good for all ages.

The length of performances varies.

Metra's UP-N train line stops at the Ravinia stop at the front gate.

Parking in the main lot is free for children's shows, $10 for classical, and $20 for pop/rock. When that lot fills up, there are park-and-ride lots that are free, with free shuttle buses, but the buses do not run for children's shows.

SIX FLAGS GREAT AMERICA

1 Great America Parkway, Gurnee, IL 60031
(847) 249-1776
http://www.sixflags.com/greatamerica
Open seasonally. Hours vary and can change. Check the website or call before visiting.

Ready to add some thrills to your summer? Fly face down and head first on Superman: Ultimate Flight; take a spin on Batman: The Ride, where the track is over your head and your feet dangle down; or try The Rage of the Gargoyles Virtual Reality Coaster. Those are just a few of the options at Six Flags Great America. There are a couple of legendary rides here too: Goliath is the tallest, steepest, fastest wooden roller coaster in the world, and the Whizzer, which opened in 1976, is an ACE Roller Coaster landmark and the only steel speed racer left. The Joker, scheduled to open in 2017, is a "free-fly" roller coaster with vehicles that will hold passengers in pairs of two on either side of the track in seats that spin all the way around. The lines, especially for popular rides, can be long on busy days, but if you purchase The Flash pass, you can reserve your spot in line and return when it's time to ride.

The big draw to Great America is the giant coasters, but kids who don't meet the height requirements definitely aren't left out of the fun. There are more than 10 rides that have no height requirements and rides with shorter height requirements including the Little Dipper, which was brought to Six Flags Great America from Chicago's Kiddieland amusement park when it closed. They've also introduced the Kid Swap program, which allows families to wait in line together, then permits one parent to ride the coaster with one child while the other stays with a second child so no one has to miss out on the big rides if one child is too small (or scared) to ride.

Season passes and memberships are available. Both have the same benefits, but the pass is a one-time fee, whereas the membership is a monthly fee. Regular price is about $190 for a season pass or $16 a month for membership. There are often sales and discounts on passes and memberships, especially during the off-season when you can sometimes get a pass for about $70 or a membership for $6 a month. Dining passes that include free drinks, lunch, dinner, and snacks during each visit are available too, as are all-season The Flash passes.

Six Flags Hurricane Harbor is a water park with 17 attractions that is attached to the park, but it requires an additional entrance fee.

Insider tip: Outside food is not allowed in the park, but you can have your hand stamped when you exit to return after eating in the parking lot.

Admission is approximately $50 online, or $70 a person at the park. Children 2 and under are free. There is an additional $8 fee for the waterpark Hurricane Harbor.

Best for ages 5 and up.

Time to explore: 3–8 hours

Pace Suburban Bus provides direct service from Schaumburg and from Rosemont to Six Flags Great America on Fridays, Saturdays, and Sundays from June to Labor Day, and every Friday and Saturday in October.

Parking is $25.

SKOKIE LAGOONS FOREST PRESERVE
1927 Green Bay Trail, Glencoe, IL 60022
(800) 870-3666
http://www.fpdcc.com/skokie-lagoons
Open sunrise to sunset daily.

If you love to get out and enjoy nature, Skokie Lagoons is the place to do it. With nearly 900 acres, there's room for everything—picnics, biking, hiking, fishing, and boating. There are seven and a half miles of trails here, most of them paved and flat, so it's easy to bring a stroller or do some easy bike riding. If you're lucky, you may catch a glimpse of ducks, herons, a minx, a fox, or other wildlife. You can launch your own boat into the lagoon or rent one from Chicago River Canoe & Kayak. Fishers can expect to find walleye, northern pike, large-mouth bass, catfish, crappie, blue gill, and bullhead here.

No admission fee.
Good for all ages.
Time to explore: 1–5 hours
The Metra UP-N train stops at the Glencoe station about two and a half miles away.
Free parking in lot.

Restaurants

THE CHOO CHOO
600 Lee Street, Des Plaines, IL 60016
(847) 391-9815
http://www.thechoochoo.com
Closed Tuesday. Open for lunch Saturday through Monday and again on Wednesday; open for lunch and dinner Thursday and Friday.

Since the early 1950s, The Choo Choo has been a favorite burger spot. There are the usual booth seats, but at the counter food is served by a train. The Choo Choo is small—there are only 45 seats in the place, with 27 of those on the tracks. The menu is simple and classic—burgers, sandwiches, and desserts—and they have a kids' menu. The restaurant has a 50s retro feel.

Be sure to bring cash, because they don't accept credit cards.

Interesting bit of trivia: The very first McDonald's restaurant opened just a few blocks away four years after The Choo Choo opened. At the time, The Choo Choo was so popular they didn't believe McDonald's would be nearly as successful. A small museum of the first McDonald's is located where the original McDonald's was, although you can only view it through the windows.

Kids' meals are about $6–$8; entrees range from about $8 to $13.
One block north of the Metra station on Lee Street.
Free parking in lot.

RAINFOREST CAFÉ
Gurnee Mills Mall, 6170 W. Gurnee Avenue, Gurnee, IL 60031
(847) 855-7800
http://www.rainforestcafe.com
Open for lunch and dinner daily.

You'll feel like you've stepped into a real rainforest at the Rainforest Café, surrounded by trees and vines. Watch for swinging (animatronic) monkeys and other creatures, including roaring lions. Suddenly, the thunder cracks and the lightning flashes and you feel like you need to run for cover as a simulated storm blows through. (Don't worry—it's just lights and sounds, no actual water.) Ribs, shrimp, sandwiches, and salads are on the menu, and they have a kids' menu with kid-sized desserts. Try out the impressive-looking Sparkling Volcano dessert, topped with real sparklers.

The gift shop here is huge with plenty of toys, clothes, and gifts. Rainforest Café has additional locations in Chicago and Schaumburg.

Entrees are in the $10–$30 range.
Pace bus route #565 stops at the Gurnee Mills Circle West/Sears.
Free parking in lot.

Free Activities

- **Emily Oaks Nature Center**—Visit this nature center in Skokie for trails, wildflowers, and a chance to see urban wildlife like great blue herons, coyotes, and Cooper's hawks.

- **Skokie Lagoons**—Skokie Lagoons covers 894 acres and offers fishing, hiking, and picnicking. Have your own kayak, canoe, sailboat, or rowboat? They can be launched here. (Rentals are available for a fee too.)

- **Bowen Park**—This Waukegan park is extraordinary, with a splash pad, tunnel slides, spider climber, and lots more.

- **Heller Nature Center**—The Heller Nature Center in Highland Park offers indoor and outdoor activities for all members of the family.

✳ NORTHWEST SUBURBS ✳

As you head into the northwest suburbs, things will get a little busier with more of an urban feel in the Schaumburg area; as you continue northwest, you'll find it to begin to turn almost rural. The northwest suburbs have plenty of U-pick places and lots of outdoor attractions. I-90, I-290, and I-294 will take you into this area, and there are several Metra trains that run here as well.

Attractions

ALL SEASONS ORCHARD
14510 IL Route 176, Woodstock, IL 60098
(815) 338-5637
http://www.allseasonsorchard.com
Open seasonally, September through October. Hours are 10:00 a.m.–5:00 p.m. on weekdays, 10:00 a.m.–6:00 p.m. on weekends.

The northwest suburbs are THE place for apple picking, and pickers come from near and far to visit All Seasons Orchard for their complete autumn experience. Visitors can choose to pay for just apple picking or the barnyard activities, but most opt for the combo experience. You can easily spend the entire day on the farm, picking from their 10,000 apple trees, navigating the three-acre corn maze, and playing in the barnyard.

There are over 30 activities on 30 acres, including things like a jumping pillow, cow train, mini zip lines, and live entertainment, but not all activities are available on weekdays. Outside food is not allowed, but the Country Kitchen serves BBQ sandwiches, burgers, and more, and dining is available indoors or at outdoor picnic tables. Pumpkins are also available at All Seasons.

Insider tip: Weekday admission is less expensive, but fewer activities are offered during the week. Arrive early, especially on the weekends, to avoid a long line and to ensure you have time to enjoy all the activities All Seasons offers.

Apple picking is about $14.50 for adults (1/2 peck of apples) and $10 for a child age 12 or younger (1/4 peck of apples). Barnyard admission is $10 on weekdays, $15 on weekends and holidays. Save money with a combo admission (apple picking plus barnyard activities) for $20.50 per adult, $16 per child on weekdays; $25.50 per adult, $21 per child on weekends.

Good for all ages.

Time to explore: 3–6 hours

Public transportation is not available nearby.

Parking in the lot is free.

DONLEY'S WILD WEST TOWN

8512 S. Union Road, Union, IL 60180
(815) 923-9000
http://www.wildwesttown.com
Open seasonally. Weekends only in spring and fall. Daily during the summer.

You'll walk into the Donley's entrance from the 21st century and be transported to the 1880s. Inside you'll find a gift shop and museum with Civil War and cowboy memorabilia, mineral mining tools and equipment, and the Streets of Yesteryear. Step out the back door into the Wild West, complete with pony rides, panning for "gold," archery, train rides, and cowboy roping.

There are a variety of rides, especially for little kids, including a small mine car rollercoaster, hand carts, canoes, and a carousel. The whole family can go for a ride on the train (which has haunted runs in the fall) and then sidle up to the bar at the saloon for some sarsaparilla.

Everything is included with the price of admission, and they have a live Wild West show a few times a day that'll knock your socks off. (Warning: There are some loud "gunshots" and "explosions" during the show that might scare sensitive kids.) Bonus: The actors do a very good job of emphasizing gun safety before each show.

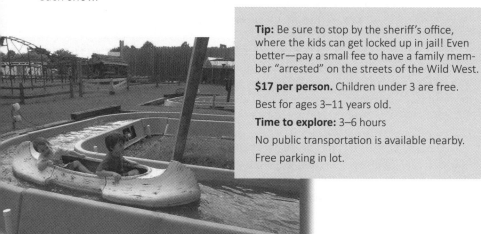

Tip: Be sure to stop by the sheriff's office, where the kids can get locked up in jail! Even better—pay a small fee to have a family member "arrested" on the streets of the Wild West.

$17 per person. Children under 3 are free.

Best for ages 3–11 years old.

Time to explore: 3–6 hours

No public transportation is available nearby.

Free parking in lot.

FIREZONE

1100 National Parkway, Schaumburg, IL 60173
(847) 824-3473
www.firezonefun.com
Office and store are open 10:00 a.m.–3:00 p.m. Tuesday through Sunday. Drop-in play days and times vary.

Firefighter is one of the most popular answers when you ask kids what they'd like to be when they grow up, and FireZone lets kids see what it's like to be a firefighter. FireZone is a business owned and operated by firefighters, and it's designed to give kids a fun place to play and learn about fire and firefighters. Kids can wear firefighter gear, slide down a pole, and play on a real fire truck and ambulance. Best of all, at the end of playtime a firefighter talks to all the kids and shows them all the gear firefighters must wear; they explain each item and put it on, allowing kids to see what a firefighter looks like in full gear with a mask so they know not to run or hide from them if there is a fire.

FireZone has drop-in play times (call or see their online calendar for dates and times), birthday party packages, field trips, and they even rent out fire trucks for parties and events.

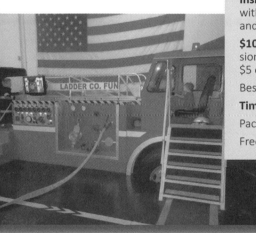

Insider tip: This is a great way to start a conversation with kids about what to do in case of emergencies and create a family fire plan.

$10 per child; children under 1 are free. Free admission for one adult with a child; additional adults are $5 each.

Best for ages 1–9 years old.

Time to explore: 1–2 hours

Pace bus route #895 stops at National/Remington.

Free parking in lot.

FOX RIVER TROLLEY MUSEUM
365 S. LaFox Street, South Elgin, IL 60177
(847) 697-4676
http://www.foxtrolley.org
Open May through October. Open on weekends and holidays; closed weekdays. Hours vary. Check website or call before visiting.

The Fox River Trolley Museum is a non-profit organization run by volunteers. They have several electric trolley cars on display, and visitors can take a four-mile, round-trip ride on a trolley along the Fox River. Trolley rides depart every 30 minutes, and you can also step onto other trolleys on display while you wait. To take the edge off, there's candy for sale in the ticket office, and a vending machine with cold drinks near the picnic table and shelter on-site. Portable restrooms are available on the grounds, or you can walk a few hundred yards to the County Park, where they have bathrooms with running water.

The Polar Express arrives in November and December, but tickets go on sale

June 1, and they usually sell out fast. Cancellations sometimes happen, so you may get to snag a couple tickets later in the year if you're really lucky.

iFLY INDOOR SKYDIVING

1752 Freedom Drive, Naperville, IL 60563
(779) 456-4359
http://www.iflyworld.com/chicago-naperville
Open Monday–Friday 10:00 a.m.–10:00 p.m., Saturday 8:00 a.m.–11:00 p.m.,
Sunday 9:00 a.m.–9:00 p.m.

If you're not familiar with iFly, the idea of indoor skydiving probably sounds pretty terrifying. However, indoor skydiving doesn't involve falling at all, just a giant vertical wind tunnel. iFly provides your flying suit, goggles, and training, and then you're off to the tunnel for your flight with the help of an instructor. Believe it or not, kids as young as 3 years old can take flight at iFly. It's pricey to fly (packages vary, but expect to pay about $70 for 2 minutes of flying time), but it's cheaper than skydiving and you spend more time in the air.

Return flight packages are a little less expensive, and you might even get a chance to learn some more advanced flying techniques. Family packages and party packages are available. iFly also has locations in Rosemont and in Chicago's Lincoln Park neighborhood.

Insider tip: You'll want a record of your flight—photographs, video, or both—so opt for a package that includes these. The photos and video taken by iFly (from inside the tunnel) will be much better than those an observer from outside the tunnel can get.

$70 for 2 flights.

For ages 3 and up.

You'll spend 1–2 hours there.

Pace route #714 stops at Diehl and Freedom, and routes #877 and #888 stop at Independence and Freedom.

Free parking in lot.

ILLINOIS RAILWAY MUSEUM

7000 Olson Road, Union, IL 60180
(815) 923-4000
http://www.irm.org
Open spring through fall, but also open for additional special events like the Happy Holiday Railway. Saturday–Monday 9:00 a.m.–5:30 p.m., Tuesday–Friday 10:00 a.m.–5:00 p.m.

Many kids (and some adults) have a fascination with trains, and the Illinois Railway Museum will delight them and maybe even create new train fans. Massive barns contain hundreds of locomotives and cars, as well as other railway memorabilia like signals, tools, signage, documents, and uniforms. The Illinois Railway Museum is the largest railway museum in the United States and is also recognized as a top-quality preservation and restoration group. They have a number of special cars and locomotives, including historic CTA transit vehicles, the *Nebraska Zephyr,* "Russian" locomotives (made for Russia but not delivered), and an Electroliner. There are 11 different collections here, but because of limited space and restoration and operational needs, they are not arranged together.

Besides just looking at trains and memorabilia, guests get a chance to take rides as well. Electric cars, steam trains, diesel trains, and trolley buses make runs, but there are different operating schedules, so you'll have to visit multiple times to try them all. The Illinois Railway Museum has a restaurant on-site and a gift shop. They also have a variety of special events throughout the year.

The Illinois Railway Museum hosts a Thomas the Train event every summer. They are also just five miles from Donley's Wild West Town.

Insider tip: The Illinois Railway Museum hosts the Day Out with Thomas in the summer. If you plan to attend, get a spot on the middle or back of the train so you can see the Thomas engine out the window when you go around the bends.

$10–$14 for adults, $7–$10 for children. Family maximum is $38–$50.

Good for all ages.

Time to explore: 2–5 hours

There is no public transportation available nearby.

Free parking in lot.

LEGOLAND DISCOVERY CENTER

The Streets at Woodfield, 601 N. Martingale Road, Schaumburg, IL 60173
(847) 592-9700
http://www.legolanddiscoverycenter.com/chicago
Open 10:00 a.m.–7:00 p.m. daily in spring and summer. Open Monday–Friday
10:00 a.m.–7:00 p.m., Saturday and Sunday 10:00 a.m.–7:00 p.m. in fall and
winter.

Is there anyone who doesn't love LEGOs? Of course not.

From the giant giraffe named Le-La who guards the entrance to the giant
selection of sets and accessories available in the gift shop, it's all LEGO all the
time at LEGOLAND Discovery Center. LEGO Master Builders (yes, it's a real job)
have created a scaled down version of downtown Chicago, construction sites,
animals, and lots more throughout the building. You'll even find some of your
favorite real and fictional people, like Einstein, Barack Obama, Harry Potter, and
Darth Vader.

Downstairs you can explore the rain forest and compete to see who can shoot
the most LEGO targets while riding on the Kingdom Quest Laser Ride. Upstairs
is the movie theater, LEGO Factory, Builder's Academy, café, and play area. Each
of the LEGO movies is only about 15 minutes long (perfect for little ones!) and
they're "4-D," so you'll feel the wind through your hair or the mist on your face
just like the characters in the movie.

The recently remodeled play area is pirate-themed and has lots of nooks and
crannies for kids to explore, and there's even a water table so kids can build and
test out LEGO boats. There's a separate area for toddlers with larger blocks and a
smaller play structure with a slide.

Of course, there are LEGOs in several areas to allow kids to build and create so
that maybe one day they can get a coveted Master Builder job!

Insider tip: Discounted tickets available online.

$18 per person. Ages 2 and under free.

Best for ages 2 to 12 years old.

Time to explore: 3–4 hours

Pace bus route #606 stops at the NW Transportation Center.

Free parking in lot.

LEVEL 257

Woodfield Mall, 2 Woodfield Mall, Schaumburg, IL 60173
(847) 805-0257
www.level257.com
Open 11:30 a.m.–11:00 p.m. Monday through Thursday, 11:30 a.m.–1:00 a.m.
Friday and Saturday, 10:00 a.m.–10:00 p.m. Sunday.

If you were (or are) a Pac-Man fanatic, you know that Level 256 is the infamous "kill screen." The screen shows a garbled mess of letters, numbers, and part of the normal game screen. Level 256 is the end; Level 257 is the "next level of play."

Level 257 is a 42,000-square-foot gaming and dining extravaganza. Wood floors, high ceilings, hanging lights, and plenty of "modern retro" Pac-Man and bowling-themed decor contribute to the upscale, trendy feel. The restaurant menu includes sandwiches, sushi, pizza, and steak, with entrees ranging from about $12 to $25. The kids' menu offers an array of choices, from $6 cheese pizza, to a $6 tofu stack, to a $15 filet mignon. Each kid's meal comes with a Pac-Man cookie. Entertainment options are plentiful—Level 257 has boutique bowling, a large arcade (including different versions of Pac-Man, of course), and even a lounge area with free board games you can play by the fire. Purchase a few Pac-Man mementos at the Pac-Shop before you go.

Level 257 is a prototype by Namco, the company behind Pac-Man, so if it's successful you can expect to see additional locations pop up around the country.

Insider tip: Level 257 can get pretty busy, so reservations are a good idea.
Cost: $5–$10 bowling per person per hour; $4 rental shoes.
Best for ages 5 and up.
Time to explore: 2–4 hours
Pace routes #208, #554, #606, #696, #757, and #906 serve Woodfield Mall.
Free parking in lot.

MCHENRY OUTDOOR THEATER

1510 N. Chapel Hill Road, McHenry, IL 60051
(847) 362-3011
http://www.goldenagecinemas.com
Open spring through fall. Gates open at 6:30; movies start at 7:30 p.m.

There are very few drive-in movie theaters left, and only two in the Chicago area. Modern theaters might boast comfy seating and great sound, but it's just not the same experience as watching a movie under the stars from your own car. Bring your own radio, use your car radio, or borrow a radio from the theater for audio. If you prefer the fresh air, spread out a blanket or take advantage of the picnic area during the flick. McHenry Outdoor Theater does a double feature every night, playing new releases as well as the occasional old favorite. You can see the schedule on their website or Facebook page as it becomes available. Movies are scheduled to run for one week. Arrive early for a good spot and bring a ball or game to play before the movie starts. If you've driven a long way to get here with young kids, it's nice to run around and get some energy out before snuggling back into the car for the movie.

Insider tip: There are many family-friendly movies throughout the summer, but only a few with a family-friendly double feature. If you've got young kids who won't doze off before the second movie starts, be sure to plan your visit during one of those showings.

$10 for an adult, $5 for a child ages 11 and under.

Good for all ages.

All shows start at 7:30 p.m., and it's always a double feature. Actual movie lengths vary.

MEDIEVAL TIMES DINNER & TOURNAMENT

2001 N. Roselle Road, Schaumburg, IL 60195
(847) 882-1492
http://www.medievaltimes.com/plan-your-trip/chicago-il/index.html
Show times are at 7:30 p.m., and sometimes at 1:30 p.m. and/or 4:30 p.m.
See website for a full schedule.

Suburban Schaumburg is not a place where you'd expect to see a giant castle, but there it is, offering guests a chance to step back into medieval times for a meal and entertainment. Medieval Times offers lunch and dinner daily, and each meal is accompanied by a tournament, which includes horsemanship, falconry, and a lively joust. Root for the knight whose section you're assigned to and enjoy the four-course meal fit for a king that is served without utensils—yep, you eat with your hands. Even the servers are dressed in medieval garb as they serve "dragon's blood (tomato) soup," "dragon scales" (garlic bread), "dragon eggs" (potatoes), "baby dragon" (roasted chicken), "dragon" corn on the cob, and "dragon claws" (dessert pastry). Although the show is the main attraction, the food is good and you get large portions. They'll wrap up leftovers in a doggy (dragon?) bag for you. Keep in mind: you're receiving restaurant-style service, so tip those serfs and wenches.

Insider tip: Go early. Seat assignments are given as you arrive, so early birds get the best seats. The lobby area contains bars, gift and souvenir shops, a photo booth, medieval displays, and a medieval torture museum, so there's plenty to do while you wait for the show to begin.

$61.95/adult, $36.95/child age 12 and under.

Best for ages 3 and up.

Time to explore: 3 hours. Shows are 2 hours long, and you can explore the castle for an hour before the show.

Pace bus route #696 stops at Roselle and Central.

Free parking in lot.

SANTA'S VILLAGE AZOOSMENT PARK

601 Dundee Avenue, East Dundee, IL 60118
(847) 426-6751
http://www.santasvillagedundee.com
Open seasonally between Mother's Day and Halloween.
Hours vary. Check website or call before visiting.

Where does Santa go every summer? East Dundee, Illinois, of course. His house is located in Santa's Village AZoosment Park, and if you're lucky you'll be able to stop in and visit for a few minutes.

Santa's Village has a long history in Chicago, and if you're native to the Chicago area, there's a good chance you visited it as a child. Originally open from 1959 to 2006, Santa's Village was purchased by new owners and reopened in 2011 as Santa's Village AZoosment Park. Rides are a mixture of old, rescued, and new attractions. Several of the rides, including Santa's Tree Slide, the Balloon Race, the Snowball Ride, and Kringle's Convoy, were part of the original Santa's Village. There are also rides from the now-defunct Kiddieland Amusement Park, like Midge-O-Racer, Space Invasion, and the Kiddie Whip Ride. New rides have been added by the new owners, including Tri-Nado, which opened in 2015, Mega Velocity and Mity Mate (2016), and the Super Cyclone, which is under construction and expected to open in 2017. There are several rides that accommodate very young children who can be accompanied by their parents.

Santa's Village AZoosment Park is intended for younger kids, from toddlers to grade schoolers, but they have rides for older kids and adults, too. Restaurants, games, and attractions like face painting and temporary tattoo booths are available as well. As you can guess from the "Zoo" in AZoosment, there is also a petting zoo. Old McDonald's Barn and Bandit's Corral are petting zoos where kids can see goats, camels, and other farm animals. Additional animal habitats can be found throughout the park, including Parakeet Paradise, Tortoise Island, and Alaskan Railway. There's a live show every day, and they still have an old favorite from the original park—the North Pole. The North Pole stands outside Santa's House, and it is a large pole of ice that remains frozen no matter how hot the weather.

Insider tip: You can often find discounts on the website or the Santa's Village AZoosment Facebook page, or on deal sites like Groupon. Santa's Village also has season passes and passes that include food and beverages.

About $25 per person. Children 2 and under are free.

Best for children ages 3 to about 10, although older children might also enjoy it.

Time to explore: 3–6 hours

Pace bus route #543 stops at Dundee/Santa's Village.

Free parking in lot.

SPRING VALLEY AND VOLKENING HERITAGE FARM

1111 E. Schaumburg Road, Schaumburg, IL 60194
(847) 985-2100
201 Plum Grove Road, Schaumburg, IL 60193
(847) 985-2102
http://www.parkfun.com/spring-valley
Grounds and trails open 8:00 a.m.–8:00 p.m. daily April–October, 8:00 a.m.–
5:00 p.m. November–March. Closed December–February.
Farm and visitor center open Tuesday–Sunday 10:00 a.m.–4:00 p.m. Closed
December–February.

These are two destinations in one—a 135-acre nature preserve and an 1880s
living history farm. Get out and enjoy some sun and fresh air on the three miles
of trails where you can observe plants and wildlife native to the area. The trails
are handicapped-accessible, so they can easily accommodate strollers too.

Volkening Heritage Farms gives visitors a glimpse of the German farm community Schaumburg was in the past. The farmers are dressed in clothes authentic
for the 1880s, and they guide visitors through the farm, where the guests help
with daily chores and participate in traditional pastimes.

In the winter, the Nature Center hosts winter festivals with crafts, snowshoe
walks, and horse-drawn wagons. In the spring (usually March), thawing begins,
and that means maple sugar. Spring Valley hosts a Sugar Bush Fair annually
so you can see how maple syrup is produced, and they also have things like
hayrides, puppet shows, and demonstrations. The fair is free, but if you arrive
early you can start the day with a breakfast of pancakes and maple syrup for only
about $5 a person.

Insider tip: Spring Valley has park packs with equipment, activities, and books to
help kids further immerse themselves in nature. Packs cost $5 to borrow for 2
weeks; call (847) 985-2100 to reserve one.

Free admission. There are fees for special events.

Good for all ages.

Time you'll spend there: 2–3 hours

Pace bus route #602 stops at Roselle and Scully, about a mile away.

Free parking in lots.

VOLO AUTO MUSEUM

27582 Volo Village Road, Volo, IL 60073
(815) 385-3644
http://www.volocars.com
Open 10:00 a.m.–5:00 p.m. daily.

Volo Auto Museum is heaven for gearheads and car fanatics, but you don't
have to be one to enjoy a visit. This 30-acre attraction has five showrooms
with famous television and movie cars, antiques, American classics, and some
crazy custom cars. You can see cars that were once owned by Oprah Winfrey,
Princess Diana, and Elvis Presley, as well as cars from your favorite movies and

TV shows—*Batman, The Fast and the Furious, Back to the Future, Knight Rider, Transformers,* and many more.

Stroll the grounds for playgrounds, antique and gift shops, and the "Military Experience" with lifelike battle scenes. Grab a slice of pizza at the diner and enjoy an animatronic show while you dine. Kids are sure to love the Flintstones car, Lightning McQueen, the Scooby-Doo Mystery Machine, and SpongeBob's Boatmobile. For a look at some of their special collection cars, purchase tickets for their historic trolley tour.

Insider tip: Volo has military displays and combat zone scenes. The combat zone scenes are dark, have an audio soundtrack to accompany the exhibit, and the scenes are realistic. It's an impressive display for mature guests, but might be scary for younger children.

$15 for adults, $9 for children ages 5–12 years old. Children under 5 are free.

Good for all ages.

Time to explore: 2–4 hours

There is no public transportation available nearby.

Free parking in lot.

YU KIDS ISLAND
Woodfield Mall, 5 Woodfield Mall, Schaumburg, IL 60173
(847) 969-9000
www.yukidschicago.com
Open 10:00 a.m.–9:00 p.m. Monday through Saturday, 11:00 a.m.–6:00 p.m.

The bright white, blue, green, yellow, and pink attractions at Yu Kids Island will catch your eye and capture the imaginations of your kids. Yu Kids is an indoor play area at Woodfield Mall, and it has the usual large play-structure maze, bouncing area, slides, and fenced play areas for little kids. However, it also has Dancing Balloons, a revolving pillow tube, a carousel, a Pillow Pool (like a waterbed for jumping), the Side Winder (a spiral-shaped playground climber), and Spinning Palms for hanging, bouncing, or swinging on.

Parents can enjoy free wifi, and there are snacks and beverages available for purchase. There is an additional Yu Kids Island location in Vernon Hills. Socks are required.

Discounted admission of $5 per child is offered during "Pajama Play," the last business hour each day. Monday through Friday after 4:00 p.m., admission is only $8 per child and $7 for siblings.

TREEHOUSE

985 S. Rand Road, Lake Zurich, IL 60047
(847) 438-8887
www.thechicagotreehouse.com
November 1–April 30—open 10:00 a.m.–5:00 p.m. Sunday through Tuesday, 10:00 a.m.–7:30 p.m. Wednesday through Saturday
May 1–August 31—open 10:00 a.m.–4:00 p.m. Saturday and Sunday; 10:00 a.m.–5:00 p.m. Monday, Tuesday, Thursday, and Friday; 10:00 a.m.–7:30 p.m. Wednesday
September 1–30—open 10:00 a.m.–3:00 p.m. Monday, Tuesday, Thursday, Friday; 10:00 a.m.–7:30 p.m. Wednesday; 10:00 a.m.–4:00 p.m. Saturday and Sunday
October 1–31—open 10:00 a.m.–5:00 p.m. Monday and Tuesday; 10:00 a.m.–7:30 p.m. Wednesday, Friday, Saturday; 10:00 a.m.–5:00 p.m. Thursday; 10:00 a.m.–4:00 p.m. Sunday

TreeHouse is an indoor play area with—you guessed it—a giant treehouse. When you enter the building, you are in the café area, with a counter and several tables. The play area is just ahead, making it easy to observe the from the café seats or from couches just in front of the play area. With 7,700 square feet of play and café space, there's plenty of room for kids to play and for parents to relax. The treehouse is part of a multi-level climbing structure with rope bridges, mats, ramps, obstacles, and slides. There's also a soft basketball court. Babies and toddlers have their own enclosed area so they can play without getting trampled by older kids. You can schedule birthday parties and special events in the party area.

TreeHouse is a peanut-free facility, and they are serious about it. No outside food or drinks are allowed in, and they do not serve anything with peanut products.

PIRATE'S COVE CHILDREN'S THEME PARK

901 Leicester Road, Elk Grove Village, IL 60007
(847) 439-2683
www.elkgroveparks.org/Pirates_Cove
Open May through September. Hours vary.

Ahoy, mateys! Avoid a mutiny from your little scurvy dogs this summer by making a trip to Pirate's Cove. Kids can captain their own paddle boat at Barnacle Bay Boats, climb the 20-foot P.J.'s Perch climbing wall, or sail through the air on a Soarin Schooner. There's also a carousel, inflatable bounce house, Pirate Plunge slide, a Castle of Camelot playground, and a train the whole family can ride. Bring your own food or purchase some at Buccaneer Bites to eat in the picnic pavilion area or on Pete's Pirate Ship. Crafts and activities are offered daily in the Galley Activity Area of Pete's Pirate Ship, and there are two shows daily Monday through Thursday at the Swashbuckler Wharf Fun Stage.

You can also purchase combo passes that get you admission to both Pirate's Cove and the Pavilion Aquatics Center. Season passes are available if you plan to visit multiple times, and Pirate's Cove is a great place for a fun-filled birthday party.

Insider tip: Save money by visiting during twilight-rate times. After 4:00 p.m. on Tuesdays and Thursdays, admission is discounted to $9 ($6 for children who are residents of Elk Grove Village). The park is open until 8:00 p.m., so there's still plenty of time to thoroughly enjoy your visit.

$12 per child; $9 per Elk Grove Village resident child. Adults are admitted free.

Recommended for children ages 1 to 9 years old.

Time to explore: 2–3 hours

Pace route #616 stops at Arlington Heights/Biesterfield/JFK about half a mile away.

Free parking in lot.

Sports

CHICAGO WOLVES

Allstate Arena, 6920 Mannheim Road, Rosemont, IL 60018
(847) 635-6601
http://rosemont.com/allstate
Season runs December through April

If you're into hockey, value for your money, and family fun, you're gonna love the Chicago Wolves. The Chicago Wolves are a professional hockey team in the American Hockey League, and they play their home games at the Allstate Arena. Notable Wolves players include Steve Maltais and Blackhawks stars Troy Murray, Chris Chelios, and Al Secord.

The show begins with "Kickstart My Heart" by Mötley Crüe playing to introduce the team, and preshow fireworks. During games you'll often see the Wolves mascot Skates and his Wolf Pack performing and pumping up the audience. Tickets for Wolves games are affordable, starting at just $11, and there are Flex Packs and Four Packs that offer discounts on multiple tickets or package deals that include tickets and concessions.

The Wolves have a variety of game day promotions throughout the season, including Star Wars Night, Adopt-A-Dog, Superhero Day, post-game autograph sessions, and lots more. Kids can join the Skate Mates Kids Club by visiting the Kids Zone near section 109 during the game.

When the Wolves aren't playing there, the Allstate Arena hosts concerts, circus performances, Monster Jam, Disney shows, and many other attractions.

Insider tip: If you're picking up tickets, Will Call is in the building across the street from the main entrance of the Allstate Arena. There are several ticket windows in the Arena by the parking lots, but these are not Will Call.

Tickets range from about $11 to $53. Children under the age of 2 are admitted without a ticket if they sit on a parent's lap.

Games usually last about two and a half hours.

Pace bus route #222 Allstate Arena Express stops at the Allstate Arena.

Parking in the lot is $15–$20.

SCHAUMBURG BOOMERS

Boomers Stadium, 1999 Springinsguth Road, Schaumburg, IL 60193
(847) 461-3695
http://www.boomersbaseball.com
Season runs from May to September.

The Schaumburg Boomers, 2013 and 2014 Frontier League Champions, play at Boomer Stadium in Schaumburg. Minor league baseball is great for families because of the lower prices and the number of family-friendly promotions they offer. At Boomer Stadium, you can purchase reserved seats or lawn seats; those sitting on the lawn can bring blankets and chairs into the stadium, although coolers and outside food is not allowed.

Friday and Saturday nights there are fireworks after the games. Sundays are Family Sundays, when you can purchase four tickets, four hot dogs, and four sodas for less than $50. Throughout the season there are special events and promotions, including things like Harry Potter Night, Squirt Gun Day, and Field of Screams. When the kids get restless during the game and need to get out a little energy, you can take them to Coop's Kids Corner, an inflatable playground area; wristbands are $5 and allow unlimited entry during the game.

Kids can join the Coop's Kids Club for free, and they'll receive a free lawn ticket to every Sunday home game, discounts, and a chance to play catch after Sunday home games.

Tickets are $7–$11. Children ages 2 and under are admitted free if they sit on an adult's lap.

Games usually last about 3 hours.

The Metra MD-W train stops at the Schaumburg station a few blocks away.

Free parking in lot.

119

Restaurants

PILOT PETE'S

905 W. Irving Park Road, Schaumburg, IL 60193
(847) 891-5100
http://www.pilot-petes.com
Open Monday–Friday 11:00 a.m.–10:00 p.m., Saturday–Sunday
11:00 a.m.–11:00 p.m.

There's delicious food at Pilot Pete's, but you may be distracted by the aviation-themed decor, including real planes suspended from the ceiling. Pilot Pete's is huge and there's a lot to look at—there's a tropical feel and the restaurant is filled with memorabilia and artifacts of air travel, including first class airplane seats, photos, and models—but the most impressive part is the wall of glass overlooking an airfield that gives you a panoramic view of the Regional Airport in Schaumburg.

The menu is extensive, including a variety of salads, calzones, Caribbean-style ribs, burgers, and sandwiches, and the prices are very affordable—most choices are $8–$15, and there's nothing over $20. Even their famous "$100 Burger" (named that because pilots will fly into the airport just to eat one) is under $10. The kids' menu includes typical kid favorites like chicken fingers and grilled cheese, and everything is less than $6.

Insider tip: Request a table near the windows so you can watch planes land and take off while you dine.

Kids' meals are $5–$6; entrees are $8–$20.

Fly in to Schaumburg airport. Metra MD-W train stops at the Schaumburg station about a mile and a half away.

Free parking in lot.

WEBER GRILL

1010 N. Meacham Road, Schaumburg, IL 60173
(847) 413-0800
http://www.webergrillrestaurant.com
Open Monday–Thursday 11:00 a.m.–10:00 p.m., Friday 11:00 a.m.–11:00 p.m., Saturday 11:30 a.m.–11:00 p.m., Sunday 11:30 a.m.–9:00 p.m.

Put down the grill tongs and basting brush and let someone else fire up the charcoal grill at Weber Grill, where 60 years of grilling experience are put to use in the open kitchen. Outside is a giant Weber Grill; inside there is a bar area and a large dining room with tables and large U-shaped booths perfect for families.

There's also an outdoor patio for dining in warm months. Steaks, ribs, chicken, burgers, and seafood are on the menu, along with salads, sandwiches, and decadent desserts. The Weber Grill kids' menu includes the old standbys (hot dog and mac n' cheese) and grilled favorites like steak skewers and BBQ Pork Ribs served on a TV tray with fruit, tater tots, seasonal vegetables, and a chocolate chip cookie.

You can hone your own grill skills by taking a grilling class. They even have a parent and child class. For $55, a parent and child (+$30 to include an additional child) will learn about grill safety and how to make hot dogs, hamburgers, and chocolate marshmallow banana boats.

If you need food on the go, you can take advantage of the "pull up and pick up" designated parking spots near the entrance. Weber Grill has additional locations in Chicago, Lombard, and Schaumburg.

Kids' meals are $7–$10. Entrees range from about $10 to $65.

Bus #895 at American Lane/Meacham or buses #554 and #696 at Meacham/American Lane.

Free parking in lot.

MILLER'S DOG N SUDS DRIVE-IN

517 Washington Street, Ingleside, IL 60041
(847) 587-6808
http://www.dognsudsdrivein.com
Open mid-March to mid-October, Tuesday–Sunday 11:00 a.m.–9:00 p.m. Closed Monday.

There are times when nothing hits the spot quite like a hot dog and frosty mug of root beer, and a carhop at Miller's Dog N Suds will deliver them carside or to a picnic table in their outdoor seating area. It's so much better than a drive thru! Kids will love having their meal delivered in a classic car box and can collect all 30 different ones. Visit on family night (Wednesday 4–9 p.m.) to meet the Miller Dog mascot and have the kids' meals at a discounted price. Special events and theme nights are scheduled throughout the summer, including Saturday night Cruise-In.

If you stop at Dog N Suds Drive-In, with locations in the north suburbs of Grayslake, Ingleside, and Richmond, be sure you try their very own Dog N Suds root beer in a frosted mug.

Insider tip: Come prepared—Miller's Dog N Suds only takes cash. If you forget, there are ATMs nearby.

A meal with a drink will cost about $8.

Take Metra Rail MD-N to Ingleside.

Free parking.

WINDHILL PANCAKE PARLOR

3307 W. Elm Street, McHenry, IL 60050
(815) 385-1172
http://www.windhillpancakeparlor.com
Open 7:00 a.m.–9:00 p.m. daily.

This McHenry gem is a bit quirky and a lot of fun. The entrance area has a plethora of gifts and goodies you can purchase and a full-size phone booth (anyone need to do a quick change à la Superman?). Windhill is decorated with countless antiques and collectibles, and the host will hand you a stack of hard-cover books when you're seated—you'll find the menu glued inside! Windhill isn't just pancakes. They offer a wide selection of breakfast, lunch, and dinner options. They decorate extravagantly for the holidays, particularly Halloween and Christmas.

There's a special surprise for the kids at the back—a small counter where a train delivers food. The train counter is small and can only seat about 10 people so if you're counting on having your food delivered by train it's best to visit during non-peak hours or be prepared to wait a while. The kids' menu has fun concoctions like a Teenage Mutant Ninja Turtle pancake.

Tuesday nights from 5:00 p.m. to 8:00 p.m. is kids' night, with a balloon artist and free kids' meals. Friday is Fish Fry night for $13.

Entrees are $9–$13.

Pace bus route #807 stops at Elm/Green and #806 stops at Richmond/Elm/Rt 120 just a couple blocks away.

Free parking.

Free Activities

- **Crabtree Nature Center**—This nature center in Barrington Hills has over 1,000 acres of woodland, wetland, and prairie.

- **Spring Valley and Volkening Heritage Farm**—Schaumburg's Spring Valley has handicapped-accessible hiking trails, a nature center, and Volkening Heritage Farm, an 1880s living history farm.

✴ WEST SUBURBS ✴

Home to lots of families and open spaces, the West suburbs has some beautiful outdoor gardens and attractions and plenty of opportunities for some retro recreation. You can reach them easily from the city via I-355, I-294, I-88, and I-55, or by Metra.

Attractions

AMERICAN SCIENCE & SURPLUS
33W361 Roosevelt Road (Route 38), West Chicago, IL 60185
(630) 232-2882
http://www.sciplus.com
Open 10:00 a.m.–7:00 p.m. Monday, Wednesday, and Friday; 10:00 a.m.–6:00 p.m. Saturday, 11:00 a.m.–5:00 p.m. Sunday.

Where can you find a periscope, miniature catapult, half of a pound of marbles, or a genuine Fallout Shelter sign? American Science & Surplus in Geneva. Although many of their items are related to science or education, the sky's the limit to what you'll find there. Surplus is the key, so expect to find great prices on weird and wacky items, but also expect that they won't last; many items are only available until they sell out, but this means every time you visit you'll make new discoveries. American Science & Surplus has additional retail locations in Chicago and Milwaukee, and an online store at www.sciplus.com.

Insider tip: American Science & Surplus occasionally has family science night events at its retail stores.
Free to browse.
Best for grade schoolers and up.
Time to explore: 1 hour or less
No public transportation is available nearby.
Free parking in lot.

BALL FACTORY

864 S. Route 59, Naperville, IL 60540
(630) 445-8365
www.ballfactoryfun.com
Open 10:00 a.m.–6:00 p.m. Sunday through Thursday, 10:00 a.m.–8:00 p.m.
Friday and Saturday.

Ball Factory is an indoor play café of epic proportions. The centerpiece is a four-level play structure with tons of obstacles and multiple slides that is large enough to be accessible by adults (in case you need to rescue a timid little one). There's also the Imagination Playground, where kids can build with giant foam blocks, and an enclosed tractor area with several ride-on toys kids can load up with "logs" and drive over the bridge or gas up at the gas pump. The Ball Blasting room is sure to be another highlight; eight floor-mounted cannons use compressed air to shoot colorful sponge balls at the floor, the wall, or an enemy (a.k.a. the kid at the gun across from you). Children under age 4 can play with foam blocks, a mini ball pit, and a small play structure with a slide in a special gated area. Parents can lounge on couches inside the gated area so they can keep a close eye on the kids.

Adults can take advantage of free wifi from the couches in the play area or the tables in the café area. The café serves wraps, sandwiches, salads, grilled cheese, and more, and pizza is available on weekends and on holidays. Outside food is not permitted. Everyone in the play area needs socks, but they can be purchased if you forget them.

$11 per child Monday–Friday, $14 per child Saturday and Sunday. Babies under 6 months and adults (13 and over) are free.

Best for children ages 6 months to 12 years old.

Time to explore: 3–4 hours

Take Pace bus route #530 or #559 to Illinois Route 59 and McCoy.

Free parking in lot.

BLACKBERRY FARM

100 S. Barnes Road, Aurora, IL 60506
(630) 892-1550
http://www.foxvalleyparkdistrict.org/facilities/blackberry-farm
Open 9:30 a.m.–2:00 p.m. Monday–Friday, 9:30 a.m.–5:00 p.m. Saturday, 11:00 a.m.–5:00 p.m. Sunday in May–October.
Open 9:30 a.m.–3:30 p.m. Monday–Friday, 9:30 a.m.–5:00 p.m. Saturday, 11:00 a.m.–5:00 p.m. Sunday in June–August; open Friday–Sunday only in September.
Open 11:00 a.m.–4:00 p.m. Saturday and Sunday in October.

Part historic reenactment, part playground, part farm, Blackberry Farm is the perfect spot to visit on a beautiful day. Seven different buildings show how families lived and worked in the 19th century—see a one-room schoolhouse, watch a blacksmith work on a forge, and see how pioneers made things like candles, soap, and butter. Then enjoy some timeless pastimes like taking a spin on the carousel, sightseeing on a train, or gliding along the water in a paddleboat.

Blackberry Farm also has the Early Streets Museum, with old-fashioned shops; the Discovery Barn, where you can see farm animals like goats, chickens, and sheep; and the Carriage House, where you can see a number of horse-drawn vehicles on display.

Finally, there's the Adventure Playground, which opened in 2013 and really is everything a playground should be. Kids (and adults) can climb up to the topsy-turvy playhouses with angled roofs and windows on multiple levels to discover what each house contains, and go up and down stairs or cross bridges that connect them. There are slides and rope ladders, and there's even a mini zip line. The playground is labeled as being best for children 5 and up, but toddlers are sure to enjoy it too, with a little more supervision and assistance.

You can bring your own food or purchase it here, and there is endless space for picnicking.

Insider tip: Leave a lot of time for the Adventure Playground—it'll be hard to drag the kids away!

$8/adult, $7/child for non-residents; residents pay $5/adult, $4.50/child. Children under 2 are free. Admission is free on Family Fun days, occurring six Wednesdays a year.

Best for children ages 3 and up.

Time to explore: 3–6 hours

Pace bus route #530 stops at Galena/Cub Foods about one and a half miles away.

Free parking in lot.

BROOKFIELD ZOO
8400 W. 31st Street, Brookfield, IL 60513
(708) 688-8000
www.brookfieldzoo.org
Open 10:00 a.m.–5:00 p.m. daily

Lions and tigers and bears—oh, my! Yep, they're all here at Brookfield Zoo. In fact, there are about 450 different species of animals from all over the world in 20 exhibits or habitats on Brookfield Zoo's 200+ acres. You can walk through the desert, the rainforest, Tropic World, the Living Coast, and the brand new Great Bear Wilderness all in one day. Brookfield has plenty of exhibits, playgrounds, and shows to keep the family entertained for the whole day. Take a spin on the carousel and tour the zoo on the Motor Safari; if you have young children, they'll love the Hamill Family Play Zoo (be sure to check out all the fun play gardens behind the building!). The Dolphins in Action show, Motor Safari tram rides, carousel, the Hamill Family Play Zoo, and Wild Encounters are not included in general admission, but are available for between $3 and $5 per person for each attraction.

There are lots of options for food in the zoo (including buffalo burgers!), or you can bring your own picnic lunch.

Insider tip: Brookfield Zoo has a small area for nursing/feeding/changing babies in the women's bathroom at the South entrance by the First Aid office; it's in the back and it's small and uncomfortable. If you can, skip it and head instead to the Hamill Family Play Zoo, where they have a large ladies' room with a changing table and a comfortable chair for feeding your baby.

Admission is approximately $18 for adults, $12.50 for children ages 3–11; children under 3 are free.

Good for all ages.

Time to explore: 3–6 hours

Pace bus route #304 stops at Washington/ Golf/Brookfield Zoo by the South entrance; bus route #331 stops at 31st/Golf View/ Brookfield Zoo near the main entrance.

Parking is $11.

CANTIGNY PARK

1S151 Winfield Road, Wheaton, IL 60189
(630) 668-5161
http://www.cantigny.org
Open 9:00 a.m.–sunset daily, November–April; 7:00 a.m.–sunset, May–October. Museum is closed on Mondays.

Cantigny Park is a large public park with a Visitor's Center, playground, restaurant, and military museum. Colonel Robert R. McCormick, a World War I veteran who fought at the Battle of Cantigny, donated his estate to become Cantigny Park. Learn about Cantigny Park in the Visitor's Center, where you can watch a short orientation film and see a 1/25 scale map of the park in the floor. Also in the Visitor's Center: a gift shop, Le Jardin restaurant, and Bertie's Coffee Shop.

Outside is a small splash fountain (although Cantigny does not allow swimsuits) and plenty of places to walk, run, and play. Cantigny has plenty of grassy and wooded areas, picnic tables, and a playground. There are two museums here—the McCormick Museum and the First Division Military Museum. The First Division Military Museum has interactive tours of war scenes. Scenes are fairly realistic and include life-size soldiers, bunkers, jungles, and bomb sounds, so you might want to skip it if you have young or sensitive children.

Whether you decide to visit the museum or skip it, the Tank Park outside is a must. There are tanks from World War I to the present, and YES, you ARE allowed to climb on the tanks!

Insider tip: Cantigny is close to Cosley Zoo, so why not plan to do both?

Free admission; just pay for parking.

Good for all ages.

Time to explore: 1–3 hours

Metra UP-W train stops at the Winfield station about one and a half miles away.

Parking in lot is $5 a car from February through December and Monday–Friday May through December; $10 a car on weekends May through September and holidays. Parking is free on the first Wednesday of each month from March through December.

CASCADE DRIVE-IN

1100 E. North Avenue, West Chicago, IL 60185
(630) 231-3150
http://www.cascadedrivein.com
Open from April to December. Open daily June through August; open weekends only in spring and fall.

Take a walk down memory lane at Cascade Drive-In in West Chicago, where you can see outdoor movies seven nights a week during the summer. Watch the daily double feature from the comfort of your own vehicle or from the heated outdoor patio. Cascade Drive-In is one of only two drive-in movie theaters remaining in the Chicago area, and it's the largest in Illinois, with parking for over 1,200 cars. Cascade has been open since 1961, and it's perfect for a night of nostalgia and modern conveniences. They have digital projection, stereo radio sound at 88.5 FM or through in-car speakers (or rent a portable radio for $1), and a full-service concession stand. There's a playground for kids, picnic area with BBQ grills, and pets are welcome. Cascade is open rain or shine and you can bring in food (as long as it's not from Scooby's).

Insider tip: Don't bring food or snacks from the nearby Scooby's Hot Dogs; there's a feud between Cascade Drive-In and Scooby's over parking lot lights, and Scooby's food is not allowed in. No joke.

Admission is $10 for adults, $5 for children ages 5 to 11 years old. Children under 5 and pets are free.

Good for all ages.

Movie times vary.

CERNAN EARTH & SPACE CENTER

Triton College, 2000 5th Avenue, River Grove, IL 60171
(708) 583-3100
http://www.triton.edu/CERNAN/
Open 9:00 a.m.–4:00 p.m. Monday–Thursday, 9:00 a.m.–1:00 p.m. Friday, 6:30 p.m.–9:30 p.m. Saturday, 1:30 p.m.–4:00 p.m. Sunday. The Cernan Center Office is typically closed on Fridays in June and July.

   The Cernan Earth & Space Center is considerably smaller than the Adler Planetarium, but there's plenty to see here, and the prices are very reasonable. Exhibits at the Center include a facsimile of the Copernicus manuscript; Apollo artifacts, including an Apollo 10 space suit; a fossil exhibit, including the Illinois "Tully Monster"; displays about the Hubble and unmanned spacecraft; and a full-scale *Brachiosaurus* footprint. Outside is a Nike Tomahawk (a missile used to collect weather info) and an Apollo Practice Capsule.
   Cernan hosts monthly Skywatch events; the presentation starts at 7:00 p.m., and if weather permits they are followed by a free public party at 8:30 p.m., with telescopes free to use. These presentations are recommended for children 13 and up, but younger children are welcome to attend too.

Insider tip: See the movie schedule for the Dome Theater online; there are a variety of movies offered for different ages.

$8 for adults, $4 for children ages 2–12.

Best for ages 4 and up.

Time to explore: 1–2 hours

Pace bus route #331 stops at 5th/Cernan Center.

Free parking in lot.

COSLEY ZOO

1356 N. Gary Avenue, Wheaton, IL 60187
(630) 665-5534
http://www.cosleyzoo.org
Open 9:00 a.m.–5:00 p.m. daily, April–October; 9:00 a.m.–4:00 p.m. daily in November; 9:00 a.m.–9:00 p.m. during the holiday season; 9:00 a.m.–4:00 p.m. daily, January–March.

   Although not as large as Lincoln Park or Brookfield Zoo, Cosley offers a relaxed farm experience at a great price. More than 150 animals occupy the five acres, along with a learning center, play area, gift shop, concession stand, and picnic area. The inner circle of the zoo contains farm animals, but as you venture further you'll find reptiles, amphibians, more than 30 types of birds, plus bobcats, coyotes, and a red fox. As a Wheaton Park District facility, Cosley is free for residents and children and has only a small fee for non-resident adult visitors.
   Cosley offers overnight programs, birthday parties, scout events, and annual events, including a Run for the Animals every June and The Festival of Lights in December.

DUPAGE CHILDREN'S MUSEUM

301 N. Washington Street, Naperville, IL 60540
(630) 637-8000
http://www.dupagechildrens.org
Open Monday–Friday 9:00 a.m.–4:00 p.m., Saturday 9:00 a.m.–5:00 p.m., Sunday noon–5:00 p.m.

After suffering a catastrophic flood in 2015, the DuPage Children's Museum is back and better than ever. Rather than repair the damaged areas, the museum did an entire renovation, updating many of the exhibits. In the renovation, they intentionally limited exhibits to science, math, and art-focused activities.

Creativity Connections uses light and shadow to teach kids about sensory input, Make It Move teaches about motion, and the AWEsome Air exhibit allows kids to explore the power of air with stomp launchers, whirligigs, and an air tunnel. The Build It exhibit is sure to be a favorite for some kids, because they get to use real tools to build with wood. Kids can create artwork in the studio, with art projects that change weekly, and do sorting, measuring, and estimating at the Math Connections exhibit.

Kids are never too young to start learning through play at the DuPage Children's Museum. Crawlers can play with beads, blocks, balls, and shapes in the Young Explorer areas, and toddlers and preschoolers will enjoy exhibits like Make It Move, Waterways, and AWEsome Air.

The S.M.A.R.T. Café serves healthy food—free of nitrates, preservatives, and antibiotics—and they offer gluten-free and vegetarian dishes. There's also the Explorer Store, which sells toys and gifts. DuPage Children's Museum hosts a variety of events throughout the year, including Bubble Bash, live performances, parties, and Family Fun nights every Friday.

FERMILAB

Kirk Road and Pine Street, Batavia, IL 60510
(630) 840-3000
http://www.fnal.gov
Open 8:00 a.m.–4:30 p.m. Monday through Friday, and 9:00 a.m.–3:00 p.m.
Saturday and Sunday. The Lederman Science Education Center is not open on
Sunday.

Fermilab, also known as the Fermi National Accelerator Laboratory, is a
national laboratory specializing in high-energy particle physics. That might not
sound like a family-friendly attraction, but it is! Fermilab has two buildings that
are open to the public—Wilson Hall and Leon Lederman Science Education
Center. Although these are designed for field trips, they are open to the public to
explore on their own.

Wilson Hall has an art gallery on the second floor, and exhibits, displays, and
observation areas on the first and fifteenth floors. The Leon Lederman Science
Education Center has hands-on exhibits, but is not open on Sundays. You can
view a map of the Fermilab public areas online, and groups of six or more must
call to book a visit.

Free tours are offered every Wednesday at 10:30 a.m.

Fermilab hosts a Family Open House once a year, with hands-on activities,
demonstrations, and tours to entertain families while teaching science. They also
have regular Art Gallery Tours, Ask-A-Scientist events, and science lectures, so
check their activities calendar.

Insider tip: Identification is required to enter Fermilab, so be sure you have a valid
ID with you.

Free

Best for ages 5 and up.

Time you'll spend there: 1–2 hours

There is no public transportation available nearby.

Free parking in lot.

GALLOPING GHOST ARCADE

9415 Ogden Avenue, Brookfield, IL 60513
(708) 485-4700
www.gallopingghostarcade.com
Open 1:00 p.m.–2:00 a.m. Monday–Friday, 11:00 a.m.–2:00 a.m. Saturday and
Sunday

Are you a pinball wizard? Or an arcade hero? Maybe it's time to find out.
Playing *Candy Crush* on a cell phone is fun, but it just isn't the same as banging
pinball flippers to send that ball flying or wrestling a joystick to jump Donkey
Kong barrels. Galloping Ghost will make you nostalgic for your childhood, and
give kids a chance to try out some arcade classics like *Donkey Kong, Space Invaders*, and *Pac-Man*. With nearly 550 arcade games, Galloping Ghost is the largest
arcade in the United States. There's no need to fumble for coins or tokens to

play—all games are set to free play; pay $15 to enter and then you can play as many games as you want for the entire day.

Insider tip: Need a break? Hang on to your receipt while you pop out for lunch or to get some sunshine, and you can return later in the day.

Cost: $15 per person for unlimited play all day.

Best for grade schoolers and older.

Time to explore: 2–3 hours

Free parking in the lot or on the street.

GO APE ZIPLINE

Bemis Woods-South, 1100 Ogden Avenue, Western Springs, IL 60558
(800) 971-8271
www.goape.com/zipline/bemiswoods
Hours vary. Open daily June through August; open weekends and some weekdays September through December and March through May.

Everyone wants to swing from the trees like Tarzan, and now you can in Bemis Woods. Go Ape has a seven-acre course 40 feet or higher in the air. Participants face 40 obstacles, like rope ladders, bridges, spider webs, trapezes, and lots more. There are five zip lines and a "Double Tarzan Swing" that swings two people 30 feet before they land in a safety net. The course takes approximately 2 to 3 hours to complete. Participants receive a 20-minute safety session before attacking the course. Reserve your spot online and arrive a little early to ensure you get started at the correct time.

Insider tip: The course is challenging, so be prepared for a serious workout!

Cost is $57 for adults (16 and older), $37 for children ages 10–15.

Must be at least 10 years old.

Time to explore: 2–3 hours

Metra BNSF train line stops at Western Springs station, about a mile away.

Free parking in lot.

HOLLYWOOD PALMS

WestRidge Court, 352 IL-59, Naperville, IL 60540
(630) 428-5800
https://www.hollywoodpalmscinema.com/

Get ready for the Hollywood experience at the Hollywood Palms Cinema, which has a full-service restaurant, bar, and theater, all of which are decorated in classic Hollywood style. You'll enjoy your movie from a high-back executive leather chair with a table or counter to hold your drinks or food, which can be purchased from the bars outside the theater or ordered from wait staff during the show. Best of all, each of the Hollywood Palms theaters is decorated in a different theme, from The Wizard of Oz, to deep sea, to the Oscar room, giving you a theatrical experience before the movie starts to roll.

Hollywood Palms has plenty of special events, including fundraisers, celebrations for movie premieres and anniversaries, holiday parties, and appearances by cast members of some of your favorite movies.

MORTON ARBORETUM

4100 Illinois 53, Lisle, IL 60532
(630) 968-0074
http://www.mortonarb.org
Grounds open 7:00 a.m.–sunset daily. Visitor center is open 9:00 a.m.–4:00 p.m. January–February, 9:00 a.m.–5:00 p.m. March–April, 9:00 am–6:00 p.m. May–October, 9:00 a.m.–4:00 p.m. November–December.

Take a little road trip to the Morton Arboretum in Lisle, Illinois, 25 minutes from Chicago. There are 1,700 acres of trees and gardens to enjoy, and you can hike or bike on the 16 miles of trails or get lost in the 1-acre maze garden. Kids will love having plenty of free space and exploring the meadows and lakefront. Keep your eyes open because the birds, frogs, and wildlife are abundant.

The Children's Garden, intended for ages 2 and up, is enormous and has a pavilion area for picnics, a secret stream kids can splash in (bring a spare set of clothes!), a playground, treehouses, and a tadpole pond. The Children's Garden is divided into the Backyard Discovery Gardens and Adventure Woods, with a total of 10 different themed gardens, each with interactive activities.

Bring a picnic lunch (the spots for picnics are endless) or grab a bite to eat at the Ginkgo Restaurant and Café for lunch or dinner.

The Morton Arboretum is open year-round and they have special events and activities for every season, including Illumination during the winter holidays, Theatre Hikes and Trick or Trees in the fall, story times in the summer, and lots more. They also have temporary exhibits. See the online calendar for all events.

RAGING WAVES WATERPARK

4000 N. Bridge Street (Hwy 47), Yorkville, IL 60560
(630) 882-6575
www.ragingwaves.com
Open late May through early September. Hours vary; the waterpark opens at
10:00 a.m. or 11:00 a.m. and closes between 5:00 p.m. and 7:00 p.m.

Raging Waves, with 45 acres and 19 different slides, is the largest water park
in Illinois. You can't drive by Raging Waves without noticing The Boomerang. This
giant slide takes a raft of four riders down a chute that plunges them into a giant
funnel. Take a double tube down The Cyclone, where you'll be "flushed" into a
giant bowl, or try P.J.'s Plummet, a body slide 72 feet long that will have you flying at up to 40 mph.

After all that excitement, play in the sand, bob in the wave pool, or float
around the lazy river. For little ones, there's a zero-depth entry pool and a giant
play structure with mini water slides, bridges, fountains, spray guns, and a giant
bucket that dumps 750 gallons of water.

Raging Waves opens when the forecast is at least 72 degrees, but clouds,
wind, rain, and other weather conditions can also be considered when deciding
whether they will open or close. No refunds are given if the park closes, but if it's
closed for more than one hour, you can get a free ticket for a future visit. Small
lockers can be rented for $10, or get the family size for $15. Tubes are available for use for free, or you can get a $5 wristband for no-wait rental tubes. You
cannot bring in flotation devices, but complimentary life jackets are available for
use. Raging Waves has two restaurants and multiple food stands inside. Outside
food is not allowed in, but there are some picnic tables in the parking area, and
you can get your hand stamped for same-day re-entry.

Height requirements vary, but anyone 48" or taller is permitted on all slides.
There are a few slides that allow children 42" or taller to ride with a parent.

Insider tip: Gather family and/or friends and plan a day together at Raging Waves,
and you'll save lots of money. Groups of 15–50 people can purchase tickets for
50% off, making the cost only $16 per person.

$32 per person.

All ages.

Time to explore: 4–6 hours

There is no public transportation available nearby.

Free parking in attached lot. $7 preferred parking.

SCITECH HANDS-ON MUSEUM

18 W. Benton Street, Aurora, IL 60506
(630) 859-3434
www.scitechmuseum.org
Closed Sunday and Monday. Open 10:00 a.m.–3:00 p.m. Tuesday through Friday, 10:00 a.m.–4:00 p.m. Saturday.

SciTech is a science museum—designed specifically for kids—with over 200 interactive STEM exhibits. Kids can test out an echo chamber, play with an air cannon, test their pitching speed, learn about pulleys, and see what it feels like to use gloves like the astronauts wear. SciTech also has a storm chaser truck on display, and a place where kids can deliver a weather broadcast. KidSpace, on the main floor, is a large play area with giant foam blocks kids can use to build things taller than they are; there are tunnels and toys appropriate for toddlers here too.

Years ago, the SciTech Museum was starting to deteriorate a little, with some exhibits missing pieces or not working properly. Since then, it's come under new management, and this seems to have reinvigorated the museum. They've recently opened a new exhibit downstairs called Space Travels, where kids can explore the universe, and they've added a STEM lab with coding and robots. If you've been there in the past, it's definitely worth a new look.

Fox Valley residents can visit the SciTech Museum for free on the first Friday of each month from 6:00 p.m. to 8:00 p.m.

Insider tip: There's no food served here, but there are restaurants in the area, and there is a lunch-room area where you can eat if you pack a lunch.

$8 per person; children 3 and younger are free.

Best for toddlers and grade schoolers.

Time to explore: About 2 hours

Pace #524 stops at River and Benton Streets.

There is free street parking for up to 3 hours and free parking in the city lot east of the museum for up to 6 hours.

STUDIO MOVIE GRILL

301 Rice Lake Square, Wheaton, IL 60189
(630) 480-9557
http://www.studiomoviegrill.com
Movie times vary.

Movie theaters are offering more and more, with high-quality sound and picture and comfortable seating. Studio Movie Grill takes it a step further with a bar in the lobby and a full American Grill menu, and everything can be delivered right to your seat during the movie. You can buy popcorn and a fountain drink if you're in the mood for the traditional experience, or live it up by ordering ribs and a milkshake followed by a dessert of Nutella beignets while you lounge in your comfy chair with a fold-down table top. There's a kids' menu too, offering things like quesadillas, burgers, and mac and cheese.

Oh, and they have movies too. Each auditorium seats between 100 and 275 people, and all seats are reserved, so there's no need to worry about scrambling for a good seat or being split from the rest of your party. Studio Movie Grill hosts special needs screenings about three times a month, with lights turned up and sound turned down; for these showings, children with special needs and their siblings are admitted free and adults are $5 each. The Family Rewind Series shows older movies for only $3 a person, and when school is out, they have the Summer Movie Series for kids, with tickets only $1 or $2.

Insider tip: Keep in mind you'll be eating in the dark wh you decide what to order.

Tickets are usually $5–$10.75 for adults, $5–$7.50 for children.

Best for ages 4 and up.

Movie times vary.

Pace bus route #714 stops at East Loop Road and Illinois Institute of Technology.

Free parking in lot.

Restaurants

ALL ABOARD DINER
The Grove Shopping Center, 1510B 75th Street, Downers Grove, IL 60516
(630) 322-8960
www.allaboarddiner.com
Open 11:00 a.m.–8:00 p.m. Monday through Saturday, 11:00 a.m.–7:00 p.m. Sunday.

What makes a hot dog or mac and cheese even more exciting for kids? Having it delivered by model train. All Aboard serves burgers, sandwiches, salads, wraps, and desserts, and has a kids' menu. While you're waiting for your food you can play video games or check out the train display with interactive features at the front of the restaurant. All Aboard has a party room for special events, and they offer a Frequent Rider Card—get 10 punches (one each time you spend at least $20) and you'll receive a $20 gift card! Kids' meals cost $6–$7. This restaurant is not affiliated with All Aboard! in Frankfort.

Attention parents of children with allergies: All Aboard Diner is a peanut- and allergy-conscious environment.

The train only delivers to counter seats, but booths are available as well. If having the train deliver food is important, plan to visit during non-peak hours or be prepared to wait a little longer.

Kids' meals are $6–$7.

Pace bus route #834 stops at 75th/Dunham.

Free parking in lot.

2TOOTS TRAIN WHISTLE GRILL

203 S. Main Street, Bartlett, IL 60103
(630) 213-6700
http://www.2toots.com
Open Monday–Saturday 11:00 a.m.–8:00 p.m., Sunday 11:00 a.m.–7:00 p.m.

There are a lot of train restaurants in the Chicago area, but they're not all the same. 2Toots Train Whistle Grill is a train-themed restaurant offering food delivery by train at every seat. Counter or booth, the train comes to you. 2Toots also carefully selected their location to be near an actual train—the Bartlett Metra station is across the street. The food they serve is the type you would expect— hot dogs, hamburgers, and chili—but they use only 100% grass-fed, prairie-raised natural Angus beef, and their hot dogs are preservative free.

There aren't any video games here, but there is a 1950s-style mechanical horse ride with real leather reins and saddle that the kids really get a kick out of riding.

Sign up your kids for their birthday club and 2Toots will send a special postcard entitling them to a free kids' meal and a train whistle cupcake during the week of their birthday. Gluten-free food is available. There is an additional location in Glen Ellyn, and a new location coming in Naperville.

Kids' meals are about $6. Meals range from about $6 to $10.

Across from the Bartlett train station on the Metra MD-W line.

Free parking in lot.

PAPPADEAUX SEAFOOD KITCHEN

921 Pasquinelli Drive, Westmont, IL 60059
(630) 455-9846
http://www.pappadeaux.com/location/32
Open Sunday–Thursday 11:00 a.m.–10:00 p.m., Friday–Saturday 11:00 a.m.–
11:00 p.m.

Are you ready for a trip to Louisiana? Pappadeaux Seafood Kitchen will take you there with their casual, festive atmosphere, attitude, and Louisiana-style cuisine. Pappadeaux specializes in seafood—everything from shrimp and crawfish to flounder and sea bass. Fish is flown in and bread is baked fresh daily, ensuring that your meal is as delicious as it can be.

Pappadeaux is a great place to try new things (and convince kids to do the same!), but they have plenty of options for picky eaters too. The kids' menu has mac and cheese, chicken, and corn dog bites for the picky eaters, and more adventurous kids can order shrimp, fried tilapia, or a combo platter.

A band strolls through the restaurant to serenade guests, and they will even play kids songs for families. Pappadeaux also has a large patio with outdoor seating in the warmer months. Reservations are always a good idea.

Kids' meals are about $5–$8. Entrees are about $20–$50.

Pace bus route #715 stops at Cass/35th, a little over a mile away.

Free parking in lot.

SUZETTE'S CREPERIE

211 W. Front Street, Wheaton, IL 60187
(630) 462-0898
http://www.suzettescreperie.com
Closed Monday. Tuesday–Thursday 7:00 a.m.–9:00 p.m., Friday–Saturday 7:00 a.m.–10:00 p.m., Sunday 8:00 a.m.–2:00 p.m.

Ditch the jeans and t-shirts for dresses and collared shirts and spend an afternoon having tea at Suzette's Creperie. You can choose either an English Tea (with finger sandwiches) or a French Tea (with crepes or quiche). Both are three courses, so you also get scones served with Devonshire cream and lemon curd, followed by a dessert of cookies and pastries. Suzette's has a wide variety of loose leaf teas to choose from, and they also offer hot chocolate for children.

Suzette's Creperie also serves breakfast, brunch, and bistro-style entrees. They don't have a separate children's menu, but they do offer a peanut butter and jelly crepe for kids that is served decorated with whipped cream and cherries to look like a face.

Afternoon tea is about $35 for adults and $16 for children age 9 and younger.

Pace bus route #711 stops at Wesley/Hale; routes #301 and #714 stop at Liberty/Wheaton.

Free street parking is available, and there is a free parking garage hidden in a small alley next door.

TATE'S OLD FASHIONED ICE CREAM

25 S. Ashland Avenue, LaGrange, IL 60525
(708) 352-4848
http://www.tatesicecreamshop.com
Open Monday–Saturday 11:00 a.m.–10:00 p.m., Sunday 11:00 a.m.–9:00 p.m.

Ice cream parlors are automatically fun places because they serve ice cream, but Tate's is a really special place. They've been making homemade ice cream on-site for 24 years, and it's delicious. The trip to Tate's is about more than just ice cream, though; the small shop has a cozy feeling, with only a few tables and a mini table just for kids. It almost feels like you're sitting in a friend's kitchen as you chat, nibble on ice cream, and play one of the board games they keep for customer use. Tate's sells gifts and candy in the shop and they have party packages too.

Tate's Old Fashioned Ice Cream is very involved with the community, offering special events, participating in parades and other local events, and giving families opportunities to meet with costumed characters. Best of all, Tate's offers a "Craft & Scoop" deal for $5. The craft changes regularly (they've done masks, gingerbread houses, etc.) and for $5 your children get the craft supplies they need and a scoop of ice cream to eat. Fun! Follow the Tate's Facebook page to keep up with what they're doing currently.

A kiddie cone is about $3, and a triple about $6.
Across the street from the LaGrange Metra BNSF train stop.
Street parking available.

Free Activities

- **Kline Creek Farm**—Step back in time to the 1890s and spend a day on the farm in West Chicago.

- **Oak Park Conservatory**—Get back to nature in Oak Park.

- **Phillips Park Zoo**—This zoo, located in Aurora, has over 100 animals representing 41 different species. Download a scavenger hunt list on their website before you go.

- **Hidden Oaks Nature Center**—Hidden Oaks is a hands-on nature center in Bolingbrook, with a rooftop garden.

- **Naperville Riverwalk**—Enjoy the beautiful scenery and landmarks along the Naperville Riverwalk, which is also close to shopping and a library.

- **Fermilab**—Fermilab offers public tours every Wednesday, Ask-a-Scientist once a month, and special events. Visitors are also welcome to explore the ground, first, and fifteenth floors of Wilson Hall and the Lederman Science Center.

- **American Science & Surplus**—American Science & Surplus is not your ordinary store; they specialize in industrial, military, and educational items, but have a little bit of everything, from test tubes to glow-in-the-dark toys to Mr. Potato Head. Spend an afternoon browsing at their Chicago or Geneva location.

SOUTH SUBURBS

As you move south from the city, you'll notice more green space, shopping malls, and golf courses. Cook County has a tremendous amount of forest preserve land and a lot of it can be found here. Historic Route 66 ran through this area. Expressways I-90, I-94, I-80, I-57, I-55, and I-294 all run through parts of the south suburbs, and there are several Metra lines that will take you to and from the city.

Attractions

ART A LA CARTE
11209 W. 159th, Orland Park, IL 60467
(708) 403-2233
www.artalacarteinc.com
Open 1:00 p.m.–9:00 p.m. Tuesday through Friday, 11:00 a.m.–9:00 p.m. Saturday, 11:00 a.m.–6:00 p.m. Sunday; closed Monday

All children are artists, so why not give them the time, space, and supplies to stimulate their creativity, and maybe even your own? Art a la Carte in Orland Park strives to create a space to encourage the community to be part of the art world. Art a la Carte hosts painting parties for kids and adults (private and open to the public), but they open the studio every weekday from 1:00 p.m. to 6:00 p.m. to anyone who wants to explore their artistic side. Open studio artists can drop in any time during those hours, and the cost includes a 16x20 canvas and supplies. Art teachers are available during this time for assistance or advice.

Field trips, scout outings, or birthday parties can be arranged, and Art a la Carte can even come to your group with a mobile party. There are plenty of paint parties for adults too, so it's a nice place for a night out with the girls or guys or for a date night. It's BYOB, so bring a drink and some snacks.

Insider tip: Call or check the online event calendar to see what they have coming up or to book a private event.

Open studio is $20 per person; $15 per student. Paint party prices are $15–$40 per person.

Best for ages 6 and up.

1–3 hours

Pace bus route #832 stops at 159th Street and 113th Avenue, a few blocks away.

Free parking in lot.

BENGTSON'S PUMPKIN FARM AND FALL FEST

13341 W. 151st Street, Homer Glen, IL 60491
(708) 301-3276
www.pumpkinfarm.com
Open September and October only.

It's not really Halloween unless you visit a pumpkin patch to pick out your pumpkin. Bengtson's Pumpkin Farm and Fall Fest provides a day of adventure with hayrides, a pumpkin chucker, petting zoo, trains, gemstone mining, a fun barn, a haunted barn, and a playground all included in the admission price. Kids get unlimited rides on the Twirling Honey Pots, 90-foot Mega Fun Slide, Happy Swing, Flying Frogs Ride, and Frog Hopper, and everyone in the family can ride on the two trains—Hootenanny Railroad and Clickety Clack Railroad. Bengtson-ville Kids Village is a play area for the kids, complete with a fire station, play jail, and school room, and nearby seating for parents. Camel rides and pony rides are also available for an additional fee.

Food choices are plentiful at Bengtson's, with food trucks and booths offering a little bit of everything: funnel cakes, pizza, tacos, sandwiches, BBQ, grilled cheese, and much more. The Bengtson's Farm is large, so wear comfortable, weather-appropriate clothing and expect to do a lot of walking.

Insider tip: Stop by the family photo booth, where you can have your photo taken and emailed to you for free. Your picture can be a souvenir of your visit to Bengston's.

Admission is $10 Monday through Thursday, $15 Friday–Sunday, and $17 on the first three Saturdays and Sundays in October.

Good for all ages.

Time to explore: 2–5 hours

Pace bus route #832 stops at 159th/Parker Road, almost one and a half miles away.

Free parking.

BIG RUN WOLF RANCH

14857 N Farrell Rd, Lockport, IL 60441
(815) 588-0044
http://www.bigrunwolfranch.org/
Open to visitors 10:00 a.m.–4:00 p.m. only on Family Day/Open House days. See website or call for upcoming dates.

Big Run Wolf Ranch is a non-profit, federally licensed facility dedicated to conservation of and education about North American wildlife. They house a variety of wolves, a black bear, a tiger, a horse, coyotes, and a variety of small animals. When you visit, you'll drive through a suburban subdivision toward a dead end and you'll be convinced you're in the wrong place, but you're not.

Big Run Wolf Ranch has been federally licensed for 30 years and has rescued several animals from being euthanized. The Ranch is only open to the public on

Family Day/Open House dates when they offer an opportunity to see the animals up close, give educational presentations, offer food for purchase, and host other activities. Big Run Wolf Ranch also allows tent camping (no RVs) on its property. Call to reserve a camping spot.

Insider tip: Big Run Wolf Ranch is always in need of support in the form of volunteers, financial donations, or donations of items on their wish list. Kuma, the North American black bear, always appreciates donations of his favorite treat—Thin Mint Girl Scout cookies.

Admission is $6; children 2 and younger are free.

Good for all ages.

Time to explore: 2–3 hours

There is no public transportation available nearby.

Free parking.

CHICAGOLAND SPEEDWAY
500 Speedway Boulevard, Joliet, IL 60433
(888) 629-7223
www.chicagolandspeedway.com

School drop-off, soccer lessons, playdates—it seems like half of parenting is spent in the car making sure everyone gets from point A to point B safely. Ditch that minivan for the day and witness NASCAR drivers putting the pedal to the metal. Chicagoland Speedway hosts NASCAR Sprint Cup Series, NASCAR Nationwide Series, NASCAR Camping World Truck Series, and ARCA Racing Series, as well as other special events. The D-shaped track is one and a half miles long and the cars zoom past at about 200 miles per hour.

Parking here is free, but it's quite a hike from the lots to the track; shuttles are offered for some of the farther lots. Small soft coolers are allowed in, so you can bring your own drinks and snacks, and concessions are available at the track too. Rumor has it that the best seats are actually at the top of the stands where you have the best view of the whole track.

Insider tip: Bring ear protection. It's very loud, so find a comfortable pair of earplugs or earphones for everyone in the family.

Tickets start at about $15 and go up from there; kids 2–12 years old are $25 off or free in some sections for select races.

Best for grade schoolers and up.

3–5 hours

Train-to-Track transportation is available from Chicago and Joliet, with shuttle service from the train station to the track.

There are several lots around the Speedway that offer free parking.

CHILDREN'S MUSEUM OF OAK LAWN

5100 Museum Drive, Oak Lawn, IL 60453
(708) 423-6709
http://www.cmoaklawn.org
Closed Mondays. Open Tuesday–Saturday 9:30 a.m.–5:00 p.m., Sunday 10:00 a.m.–5:00 p.m. Open until 8:00 p.m. on Friday nights from October through April.

The Chicago area has several children's museums; some are very large, some are small, but the Children's Museum of Oak Lawn fits perfectly in the middle. It's small enough that kids (and parents) won't be overwhelmed, but large enough to have plenty for kids to do. There are two floors (with a safety gate at the top of the stairs) and a wide variety of educational and fun exhibits. The We the People exhibit includes two pieces of beam from the World Trade Center and focuses on unity, patriotism, and friendship. What If...? takes a look at diversity in terms of impairment, such as hearing loss, loss of vision, loss of a limb, or autism. Nanoscale: Science of Small explores particles. There's also a treehouse play area, a grocery store, a theater (with costumes, of course), a café where kids can serve (toy) foods and ice cream, and much more. Kids who love to get messy will want to check out the water table and the art area. There's an enclosed area for babies and toddlers too, with plenty of soft toys and small play structures.

Insider tip: There are a number of restaurants within walk distance of the museum, including Dunkin' Donuts, Smash burger, and Lou Malnati's, and the Oak Lawn Public Library just a few blocks away.

Admission is $9 per person; children under the age of 1 ar free.

Best for babies to children up to 12 years old.

Time to explore: 3–4 hours

The Metra SWS train stops at the Oak Lawn station; there no train on Sunday. Pace bus route #381 stops at 95th and Museum Drive.

Free parking on 5th floor of parking garage Monday–Saturday, anywhere in parking garage on Sunday.

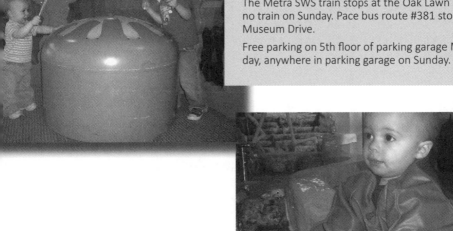

GIZMO'S FUN FACTORY

66 Orland Square Drive, Suite D, Orland Park, IL 60462
(708) 949-8948
www.gizmosfunfactory.com
Open 4:00 p.m. 10:00 p.m. Monday through Thursday, 4:00 p.m.–11:00 p.m.
Friday, 10:00 a.m.–11:00 p.m. Saturday, 10:00 a.m.–8:00 p.m. Sunday

Laser tag, rock climbing, and indoor ropes course—Gizmo's Fun Factory is an amusement park under one very large roof. This 47,000-square-foot building has 70 arcade games, seven major attractions, and seven party rooms, and that's plenty to provide hours of fun. Tinker Tot Toyland has obstacles, tube slides, a foam ball blaster, and a four-story play structure. That's likely to keep most kids busy for the day, but there's also a three-story Ratchets & Ropes course with a zip line, a laser maze where kids need to navigate an interactive floor while dodging laser beams, three climbing walls, go-karts, and Widget Whirl with spinning bumper cars. Laser tag is here too, but it's not your ordinary laser tag; here you battle a robot army in a two-story arena filled with black lights, fog, and music. Height restrictions vary for different activities; all are listed on their website.

The Gizmo's restaurant serves pizza and burgers and similar fare, and they have a kids' menu but also offer adult beverages. Don't forget your socks!

Insider tip: It's easy to spend several hours here, especially with older kids, so the 4-hour wristband is probably the most economical choice.

$28–$35 for 4 hours of unlimited play. Alternatively, you can pay for attractions individually or pay-as-you-play with a Gizmo's game card.

Best for toddlers and up.

Time to explore: 3–5 hours

Pace bus routes #364, #379, and #832 stop at the Orland Square Sears stop across the parking lot.

Free parking in lot.

HAUNTED TRAILS FAMILY AMUSEMENT PARK

7759 Harlem Avenue, Burbank, IL 60459
(708) 598-8580
www.hauntedtrailsburbank.com
Open 11:00 a.m.–10:00 p.m. Monday through Thursday, 11:00 a.m.–midnight
Friday, 10:00 a.m.–midnight Saturday, 10:00 a.m.–10:00 p.m. Sunday. Open
10:00 a.m.–midnight daily from June through August.

Every day is Halloween at Haunted Trails Family Amusement Park in Burbank. Haunted Trails has been a popular spot for mini golf, batting cages, and arcade games for decades, but over the years they've expanded to add go-karts, rides, and a restaurant.

Golf alongside (statues of) ghosts and ghouls, and work your way over to the haunted castle. The fear factor here is pretty low as the creatures are reminiscent of Scooby Doo villains. Adults and big kids can take a spin around the go-kart track or in the Tornado ride. Little ones (3 and up) can ride the Miner

Mike Coaster, and parents can ride along too. There's a Jr. go-kart track for kids 4 and up.

There are two arcades here: The one by the mini-golf course has the more traditional video games, whereas the larger Monster's Tomb Game Room has skill and sport games where you can earn tickets for playing. If you'd like more active games, try out Lazer Frenzy, where you have to complete tasks without touching any of the laser beams surrounding you. When you start to hear growling (in your stomach), grab a seat at Charmin' Charlie's for a pizza.

Haunted Trails cranks up the spookiness in October with the Frightmare Haunted House—a two-story twisted maze of scary fun. The haunted house costs about $12 per person. Too scary for the little ones? Inquire about the kids' matinee, with the lights on and a lower ticket price; this is usually offered as part of a kids' fun fest just before Halloween.

Haunted Trails is open year-round, and they often have specials and holiday events listed on their website. Birthday parties and special events can also be arranged.

KIDSWORK CHILDREN'S MUSEUM

11 S. White Street, Frankfort, IL 60423
(815) 469-1199
http://www.kidsworkchildrensmuseum.org
Open Tuesday–Friday 9:00 a.m.–3:00 p.m., Saturday 9:00 a.m.–4:00 p.m., Sunday 11:00 a.m.–4:00 p.m. Open 9:00 a.m.–3:00 p.m. on school holidays.

KidsWork is a little smaller than some of the other children's museums in the Chicago area, but it has impressive exhibits, and it's a little easier to supervise the little ones there. KidsWork occupies a two-story space in the historic downtown Trolley Barn in Frankfort. The theme of the first floor is "Science in Action." A 3-D full body Pin Screen, a touchscreen SMART table, and a sensory table are on this level. Additionally, kids can be a pet vet to stuffed animals, build with blocks, man a 911 center, and dig for dinosaur bones. The Tot Spot is also on the first level. This is an enclosed area with soft toys, a small play structure with a slide, and toys appropriate for babies and toddlers.

Upstairs the theme is "Creativity Abounds." There's a reading area, musical instruments, an exhibit exploring lights and shadows, a sensory table, and face painting. There's also Imagination Theater, a large stage with puppets and costumes so kids can put on a show, and the ArtWorks area with paper, paints, markers, scissors, and glue. There's a safety gate at the top of the stairs so parents don't need to worry about little ones falling down the stairs or escaping.

Also in the Trolley Barn: Kernel Sweet Tooth (selling popcorn and sweets), Downtown Guitars, and White Street Café, which serves breakfast, lunch, and dinner.

Insider tip: Strollers are inconvenient here; there's a spot to park them near the coats. If you must have one, there's a wheelchair elevator to use to get to the second floor.

$7 per person. Children under 1 are free.

Best for children ages 1 to 8.

Time to explore: 2–3 hours

There is no public transportation available nearby.

Free parking in lot.

LAKE KATHERINE NATURE CENTER AND BOTANIC GARDENS
7402 Lake Katherine Drive, Palos Heights, IL 60463
(708) 361-1873
http://www.lakekatherine.org
Park is open dawn to dusk. Nature Center open Monday–Friday 9:00 a.m.–5:00 p.m., Saturday 10:00 a.m.–4:00 p.m.; closed Sunday.

Lake Katherine is a non-profit, 85-acre park that includes wetlands, woodlands, gardens, prairies, and a 10-acre lake. Inside the Nature Center there are games, crafts, areas to play, and hands-on animal encounters for children. Children's programs and special events are available year-round, including fireworks for the Fourth of July, fishing fundraisers, a Monarch butterfly festival, and Winterfest. There is a free story time once a week, and a variety of classes for kids that are only $6; registration for these classes is required.

Outside there are six miles of trails, a waterfall, an arboretum, several gardens, and a Children's Forest with wetlands, a schoolhouse arch, a spider maze, a salamander mound, and other fun things to do. Pets are allowed at Lake Katherine, but biking, fishing, swimming, and picnicking are not. There are several restaurants nearby. Canoes and kayaks can be rented for $8 per person per hour.

Park personnel at Lake Katherine dye the waterfall green for St. Patrick's Day each year, and it's a really fun celebration for younger kids.

Insider tip: The paths are not very accessible for the handicapped or regular strollers. If you're bringing a baby, you're better off with a baby carrier or a jogging stroller.

Free

Good for all ages.

Time to explore: 2–3 hours

Pace bus route #386 stops at Harlem and College Road.

Free parking in lot.

LITTLE RED SCHOOLHOUSE NATURE CENTER

9800 Willow Springs Rd, Willow Springs, IL 60480
(708) 839-6897
http://www.fpdcc.com/nature-centers/little-red-schoolhouse-nature-center
Grounds open 8:00 a.m.–5:00 p.m. March–October and 8:00 a.m.–4:00 p.m.
November–February.
Nature Center open 9:00 a.m.–5:00 p.m. March–October, 9:00 a.m.–4:00 p.m.
November–February.

In the 1880s a small schoolhouse was built to teach community students; 80
years and two moves later, the schoolhouse became the Little Red Schoolhouse
Nature Center, and rather than continue teaching reading, writing, and arithme-
tic, it was filled with nature displays and fish tanks to teach visitors to the forest
preserve about nature. In 2010, the exhibits and animals were moved to a new,
much larger building. The historic schoolhouse remains, but the new visitor's
center is where you want to be.

The Little Red Schoolhouse Nature Center is surrounded by forest where there are
trails for hiking. There is a short path near the visitor's center—perfect for a short
walk with the kids—that goes past the pond, beehives, and a small shelter overlooking the lake. There are lots of animals to see: plenty of fish, birds, and frogs.

Inside you'll find live animals, including birds, fish, spiders, and snakes; interactive displays that teach about animals and nature; and a turtle pond area. A
ramp walkway leads down to the fish and pond displays. The walkway is divided
into different time periods, with dinosaur footprints on the walkway so kids can
see the progression of nature from dinosaurs to modern man. There is also a
large Montessori play area that includes a table for crafts and coloring, a sensory table, small tents for the kids to play under, and sticks to build a campfire.
There's a family bathroom here as well.

Insider tip: The Plush Horse ice cream parlor is
just a short drive away, and it's a perfect place
to enjoy a cold ice cream cone after a hot day in
the forest.

Free

Good for all ages.

Time to explore: 2–3 hours

There is no public transportation nearby.

Free parking in lots.

PICK. AT GARDEN PATCH FARMS

14158 W. 159th Street, Homer Glen, IL 60491
(708) 301-7720
http://www.pickthefarm.com
Store open year-round; fields open seasonally. During the summer, field hours
are 9:00 a.m.–6:00 p.m. daily.

Sometimes you want something more than the standard Gala, Red Delicious,
or Honeycrisp apples, and that's when it's time to hit Pick. at Garden Patch
Farms. Not only do they have 60+ varieties of apples and pears, but you can
also pick blackberries, grapes, raspberries, and more fruit, as well as 40 types of
vegetables—everything from eggplant, to okra, to rhubarb—on their 30 acres.
There is a $5 field charge per person, and after that you pay for what you pick
by weight. Wagons are available to help lug your picks (or kids!) in and out of
the fields. Stop by the shop to pick up harvested produce, eggs, or snacks, or for
some feed corn so you can feed the chickens. Check what's in season for picking
and the cost of each item per pound on their website.

Pick. At Garden Patch Farms hosts an annual Butterfly Festival in April. Face-
painting, a bounce house, and crafts are generally available during the festival,
and they do a butterfly release twice—once in the morning and again in the
afternoon.

$5 admission fee to enter fields; produce is
priced by pound.

Good for all ages.

Time to explore: 1–4 hours

Pace bus route #832 stops at 159th/Messenger.

Free parking in gravel lot.

Sports

CHICAGO FIRE
Toyota Park, 7000 Harlem Avenue, Bridgeview, IL 60455
(708) 594-7200
www.chicago-fire.com
Season March through October

You gotta love a sports game that starts with a party! The Chicago Fire, a major league soccer team, hosts the Fire Fest, a pre-game celebration that begins two and a half hours before every home game. Music, games, and prizes—along with mascot Sparky the Dalmatian—get fans excited and ready to cheer the team on to victory.

The Chicago Fire also has a charitable organization, the Chicago Fire Foundation. Through the Foundation, they offer soccer skills training to children, accept donations of gently used sports equipment for sports teams, and provide tickets to games for non-profit youth organizations.

Kids who love the Chicago Fire can be Junior Supporters. This free membership entitles them to special ticket offers, e-newsletters, and an invitation to an autograph session. For a $30 membership fee kids get the same benefits but also receive Chicago Fire merchandise. For kids who want to be more involved and play soccer, the Chicago Fire has the Little Sparks program for kids 2 to 5 years old, and the Chicago Fire Juniors, as well as summer camp programs.

Cost: $20.
Games are about 2 hours long.
Toyota Park Express runs 2 hours before games and 30 minutes after between the Orange Line Midway station and Toyota Park.
Parking is $20.

WINDY CITY THUNDERBOLTS
Standard Bank Stadium, 14011 South Kenton Avenue, Crestwood, IL 60445
(708) 489-2255
http://www.wcthunderbolts.com
Season runs from May to September.

Baseball is America's favorite pastime, and it's a great family outing, but visiting a minor league team has certain advantages, too, especially when you have young children. They're often not as crowded as major league games, they're cheaper, the players are often more accessible, and the teams often cater to families. This is definitely the case with the Windy City Thunderbolts. The Thunderbolts play a great game of baseball, but that's not the only thing going on at Standard Bank Stadium. Special events and promotions mean some days there will also be a petting zoo, or even a Pro Wrestling Blitz after the game.

Take advantage of "$2 Tuesdays" to get tickets for—you guessed it—only $2, or visit on Sunday for Family Day, when you can purchase four tickets, four hot dogs, four chips, four sodas, and four Thunderbolts hats for only $50. There are fireworks on Fridays and Saturdays, and when there aren't fireworks, kids are invited to run the bases after the game.

Kids can join the Boomer's Buddies fan club for free and receive a t-shirt, autographed photo of Boomer, a birthday e-card, free admission to every Sunday home game, and invitations to special events on Sundays.

Tickets are $7–$11. Children ages 3 and under do not require a ticket if they sit on an adult's lap. Tickets on "$2 Tuesdays" are only $2.

Games last about 3 hours.

Pace bus route #383 stops at Cicero/141st a few blocks away.

Parking in the attached lot is $2.

Restaurants

ALL ABOARD! FAMILY DINING AND AMUSEMENT

20831 S. LaGrange, Frankfort, IL 60423
(815) 806-9005
http://www.allaboarddining.com
Open Monday 11:00 a.m.–3:00 p.m., Tuesday–Wednesday 11:00 a.m.–7:00 p.m., Thursday–Saturday 11:00 a.m.–8:00 p.m., Sunday 11:00 a.m.–5:00 p.m.

Childhood and trains just seem to go together, and the owners of All Aboard! sure do agree. Originally Choo Choo Johnny's, this restaurant changed its name when the new owners bought it, and it serves hot dogs, sandwiches, salads, and wraps delivered to the counter seats by a train. All Aboard! also has some video games, a giant painting of a train on one wall, tables away from the counter, and a model train set up at the front of the restaurant that has buttons kids can press to control parts of the model town.

In case that's not quite enough entertainment, there's a playroom in the back for kids between the ages of 1 and 7. A ride-on toy train, train table, chalkboards, and blocks will keep the kids busy while waiting for food or help burn off a little energy after they eat. The playroom can also be used for birthday parties.

Kids eat free on Tuesday nights from 3:00 p.m. to 7:00 p.m., and Thursday is "Grannies & Nannies Day," when grannies and nannies receive 15% off their bills. Check out their website for coupons.

Note: This restaurant is not affiliated with the All Aboard Diner in Downers Grove.

Kids' meals range from $5 to $7. Entrees are $5–$12.

There is no public transportation available nearby.

Free parking in lot.

CHUCK'S SOUTHERN COMFORTS CAFÉ

6501 W. 79th Street, Burbank, IL 60459
(708) 229-8700
http://www.chuckscafeburbank.com
Open for breakfast, lunch, dinner, and late-night dining daily.

Southsiders have a secret—Chuck's Southern Comforts Café. Blending Mexican, Cajun-Creole, and Southern BBQ, Chuck's creates amazing meals for breakfast, lunch, and dinner. Chuck—whom you'll often see checking in on tables—received training from Rick Bayless before opening Chuck's. In the beginning, it was a tiny little place in a strip mall, but as the word got out they had to move to the much larger current location. Chuck's has been featured on local and national television shows, including *Check, Please!, Windy City Live,* and *Diners, Drive-ins, & Dives.*

The dining room is warm yellow and orange with a mixture of Southwest/Mexican/Mardi Gras decor. Their menu is huge, so if you have difficulty choosing, you can't go wrong with the Super Sampler or BBQ Combo; both are around $20 and come with a huge variety of food so you can try multiple food items. You'll have plenty to bring home too! Chuck's is the kind of place where you can feel comfortable and relaxed, enjoy spending time with your family, and eat some really good food. They have a gluten-free menu, and they're more than just great BBQ—they also offer soup and fantastic breakfast options. Chuck's celebrates Mardi Gras and Cinco de Mayo with special dishes and has special events throughout the year. There is an additional location in Darien.

Kids' meals are $5–$8; adult entrees are $8–$25.
Pace bus stops at the corner of 79th and Natchez.
Free parking in lot.

THE PLUSH HORSE

12301 S. 86th Avenue, Palos Park, IL 60464
(708) 448-0550
http://www.theplushhorse.com
Open year-round.
Open Monday–Saturday 8:00 a.m.–10:00 p.m., Sunday 11:00 a.m.–10:00 p.m. during the summer.

I scream, you scream, we all scream for ice cream! Sure, that pun's old, but it sticks around because it's true. Who doesn't love a giant scoop of heaven in a cone? The Plush Horse in Palos Park has been making and scooping ice cream for about 75 years, so they've really perfected the craft. They'll have you feeling nostalgic whether you visited there as a child or not, with wood floors, pendant lights, a carousel horse, a life-size plush horse, and a miniature ice cream parlor table and chair set for little kids.

You can choose from over 40 flavors of homemade ice cream, with everything from Superman to Pumpkin Pie to Egg Nog. They often have specialty flavors as well, such as CUBoom! after the Cubs won the World Series (peanuts and Cracker Jack in a caramel swirl) and Sheri Potter (butter beer and rum). Not sure if you'll like a flavor? Ask for a sample before you order.

Of course, there are almost as many ways to eat your ice cream as there are flavors; you can get it in a cup or cone, as part of a sundae or banana split, in a waffle cone, a flavored waffle cone (red velvet, peppermint, or chocolate hazelnut, to name a few), or in an espresso float. The Plush Horse has ice cream cakes, too, if you want to take one home for a celebration (or just because)!

When placing your order, keep in mind they tend to scoop big, so a single scoop is really more than just one scoop. Pony cones are available for kids. Enjoy your scoop(s) in the old-fashioned ice cream parlor or in the large courtyard outside. As you'd expect, The Plush Horse gets busy, especially on hot days, so don't be surprised if there's a long line, and as there are only a few tables inside, you should plan to eat outside. The Plush Horse has a Little Free Library in their courtyard, so bring a book to leave and maybe you'll find something good to read in exchange.

A single scoop is about $3.50.

The Metra RI train stops at the Tinley/80th station about one and a half miles away.

Free parking in lots or on street.

POLK-A-DOT DRIVE IN
222 N. Front Street, Braidwood, IL 60408
(815) 458-3377
Open for lunch and dinner daily.

Grab your camera or your cell phone and strike a pose with the life-size statues of Marilyn Monroe, Elvis, James Dean, the Blues Brothers, and Betty Boop outside the Polk-A-Dot Diner. The diner opened in the 1950s and has hung onto the 50s and Route 66 themes. Inside there's a black-and-white tiled floor, vinyl booths, Betty Boop decor, and a kiddy car ride. Polk-A-Dot is so retro that they don't even have a website. They do have a pay phone hanging on the wall and an old-fashioned juke box that plays actual records.

Polk-A-Dot Drive In serves your favorite greasy and deep-fried foods—pizzaburgers, corn dogs, fried chicken—and their specialty is chili cheese fries.

Although the prices might not be from the 1950s, they're definitely less than you'll pay at most places today. You'll pay less than $10 for a meal. And those chili cheese fries everyone loves? Only $4 for a large order. Grab your poodle skirts and leather jackets and hit Route 66 for this retro treasure.

Kids' meals are less than $4 and include a drink; dinners are $7–$8, and sandwiches or burgers are $2–$5.

Public transportation is not available nearby.

Free parking lot.

WHITE FENCE FARM

1376 Joliet Road, Romeoville, IL 60446
(630) 739-1720
www.whitefencefarm-il.com
Open for dinner Tuesday through Saturday, and for lunch and dinner on Sunday. Closed Monday.

When you arrive at White Fence Farm, you're greeted by a giant rooster statue outside; inside, White Fence Farm is like an old-fashioned supper club, complete with live music on select nights and plenty of kitschy decor. It's a mini-museum of antique cars, vintage toys, and other memorabilia.

There are plenty of options on the menu—several kinds of steak and sea-food—but fried chicken is their specialty and has been since they opened in the 1920s. In fact, they claim it's the World's Greatest Chicken. Along with your meal they serve a wide selection of relishes, family-style: pickled beets, kidney bean salad, coleslaw, corn fritters, and cottage cheese. Dinners also include a brandy ice dessert.

There's a petting zoo behind the restaurant, with alpacas, goats, and chickens; however, they're fenced in, and it may be difficult to actually pet them. It may be a little weird to feed chickens before they feed you, but the kids will love it.

A kid-sized portion is $7. Entrees are about $11–$35.

Pace bus routes #850 and #851 stop at the White Fence Farm stop.

Free parking in lot.

Free Activities

- **Lake Katherine Nature Center and Botanic Gardens**—You'll love the scenery and nature center at Lake Katherine. (And keep it in mind in March for the Dyeing of the Waterfall!)

- **Little Red Schoolhouse Nature Center**—Walk the trails outside, or get involved in interactive activities and see some animals inside the nature center in Willow Springs.

★ SEASONAL FAIRS, FESTIVALS, AND EVENTS ★

Some of the best family attractions in Chicago are, unfortunately, only temporary. Fairs, festivals, and events are taking place every week of the year all over the city. Chicago's diversity is reflected in the array of events, from ethnic and cultural celebrations, to charity functions, to seasonal performances.

CHICAGO AUTO SHOW

McCormick Place, 2301 S. King Drive, Chicago, IL 60616
www.chicagoautoshow.com
Takes place in February and is open to the public for 9 days.

You don't need to be a car aficionado to appreciate the Chicago Auto Show, the largest car show in North America. With one million square feet of space and over 1,000 cars on display, you can check out cars of every size, shape, and type. Check out new looks and features, and take an opportunity to sit in your favorite car. (Bonus: It's hard to do much walking in the winter months, but you'll make up for it here!) Competition vehicles, antique cars, and collector cars are also on display at the Chicago Auto Show, and there are a number of vendors selling auto-related products. You might even be able to perform a good deed (donate blood) or complete a mundane errand (renew your driver's license) while you're there.

Each year the Chicago Auto Show hosts a Family Day with special programs geared toward children and families. Kids can learn about the process of making a car from design to manufacture, enjoy some interactive demonstrations, and maybe even take a spin on a course in a kids' motorized car.

There's also a Women's Day, with discounted admission for women ($7 instead of $13) and many of the car companies and vendors cater to women, offering demonstrations, special guests, and presentations.

Expect lots of special guests and maybe even performances at the Auto Show. In the past, some car manufacturers have staged concerts or offered an opportunity to drive a vehicle on an indoor course. There are plenty of food vendors, and you are also allowed to bring your own food into the show.

Insider tips: Use the coat check (the fee is about $3) so you don't need to lug around winter gear, pack some snacks and some water, and bring a stroller or baby carrier for very young children, because it's a lot of walking.

Admission is $13 for adults, $7 for children ages 7–12; children 6 and under are free with a paid adult family member.

Best for ages 5 and up.

CTA bus routes #3 and #21 stop at McCormick Place, and the Metra Electric and South Shore train lines stop at the McCormick Place station.

Shuttle buses from area parking lots, where parking is about $15–$20. During the weekend, there are also shuttles from Millennium Park and East Monroe underground garages.

MONSTER JAM

Allstate Arena, 6920 Mannheim Road, Rosemont, IL 60018
www.monsterjam.com
Arrives in February for 6 shows in 3 days.
On a SUNDAY! SUNDAY! SUNDAY!! (and also Friday and Saturday) in February

Monster Jam makes its annual appearance in the Chicagoland area. Monster Jam legends, like Grave Digger, El Toro Loco, Zombie, Monster Mutt Rottweiler, and Megalodon, will be there with engines roaring racing around the track, crushing cars, and flying up and over a variety of ramps and obstacles. Whether you're a die-hard monster truck fan or new to the entire experience, it'll be an entertaining show.

Monster Jam is a very popular event, so it's best to purchase tickets early and bring ear protection, especially for the kids. It's incredibly loud, so ear protection is a good idea for everyone in the family. They do sell disposable ear plugs and novelty ear protection (headphones shaped like monster tires) at the event, but you'll definitely pay more and have to wait in line.

Select performances offer a Pit Party before the show, with a chance for visitors to get up close and personal with the drivers and the trucks. The Pit Party lasts one and a half hours and during that time you can talk to drivers, see the trucks up close, and request autographs. Tickets for the Pit Party need to be purchased in addition to Monster Jam show tickets, and they cost about $10 a person; children under 2 are admitted free with a ticket-holding parent.

A word of warning for young or sensitive children: Monster Jam can be scary. It's loud, there are pyrotechnics, and the trucks fly in the air and sometimes crash. Some kids think it's exciting, while others think it's scary, so decide beforehand if this is the right kind of event for your child.

Tickets start at $22. Children under 2 are admitted free if they sit on a parent's lap.

Best for ages 3 and up, but it may be too loud or too scary for some children.

Pace bus route #250 stops at Mannheim/Lunt/Allstate Arena. Additional Pace bus routes also stop nearby on Touhy, on Maple, and on Higgins.

Free parking.

TRITON TROUPERS CIRCUS

Triton College, Robert Collins Building, 2001 N. Fifth Avenue, River Grove, IL 60171
http://tritontrouperscircus.com/
Thursday, Friday, and Saturday one week before Easter each year.

There's nothing that brings out the kid in all of us like a circus. If you love the circus but not the price tag or the crowds, the Triton Troupers Circus is for you. The Triton Troupers Circus is a non-profit organization dedicated to preserving the circus arts, and they train just outside of Chicago at Triton College in River Grove. The Triton Troupers are a dedicated group of adults and children who spend their spare time training in circus arts, and every year since 1972 long hours of training and practice culminate in a series of performances held the week before Easter. The venue, crowd, prices, and difficulty of the stunts are smaller than you'd find at a major circus, but this is what makes it especially family-friendly. All shows are handicapped accessible, animal-free, and appropriate for all ages. Expect balloons, fog, confetti, and strobe lights during the show. The Troupers schedule one show to be interpreted for the hearing impaired.

The Triton Troupers also host a fundraising pancake breakfast, usually the morning before the Saturday performance, from about 8:00 a.m. until noon. In past years, the breakfast has included all-you-can-eat pancakes, sausage, coffee, juice, and milk for only $4 ($5 at the door), or $8 ($10 at the door) for the breakfast and circus admission.

Tickets are only $6 per person, and they can be purchased at practices, at the Office of Student Life building during school hours, or at the show, which takes place in the Robert Collins Building at Triton College. Doors open 1 hour before showtime, but the clown show begins right away, with clowns interacting with attendees, painting faces, and performing silly tricks. Drinks and snacks are available for purchase at the show at very reasonable prices. The best part about the Triton Troupers is that these are normal people from the community living out their dream and entertaining families.

Be sure to arrive an hour early to interact with the friendly clowns and for some preshow entertainment!

$6 per person
Good for all ages; best for toddlers through grade schoolers.
Two-hour show; optional hour preshow.
Pace bus route #331 stops at Triton College.
Free parking in attached lot.

FAIRY FEST AT PILCHER PARK

Pilcher Park Nature Center, 2501 Highland Park Drive, Joliet, IL 60432
http://www.jolietpark.org/jpdj/index.php/programs/special-events
Takes place in May for one day

Childhood is a time to believe in magic and fairies. Each Spring, as flowers are blooming and nature is waking up after a long slumber, fairies of all ages come to Pilcher Park Nature Center. The annual Fairy Festival invites families to become fairies. The day begins with an enchanting Breakfast with the Fairies, where winged hostesses will sprinkle magical fairy dust on guests and pose for photos. After breakfast, guests will be given a fairy name and invited to create magic wands and wings. Visiting fairies can participate in the Fairy Flight Simulator, learn secret magical powers (like invisibility!), and take the Fairy Pledge at Fairy School.

Come dressed for the occasion! Wear wings, a dress, or other magical garb to frolic with the fairies.

Admission is $10 per person. An optional breakfast is an additional $5 per person.
Best for ages 3 and up.
Pace bus route #508 stops at Briggs/Cass, a little over a mile away.
Free parking.

CHICAGO KIDS & KITES FESTIVAL

Cricket Hill at Lincoln Park, near the intersection of Lakeshore Drive and Montrose Avenue, Chicago, IL 60640
http://www.chicagokidsandkites.us/
Takes place in early May for one day

Spring means it's time to go fly a kite! Chicago hosts a Kids & Kites Festival each year at Lincoln Park, offering families a chance to get out and enjoy the warming weather. The festival is free, and the city of Chicago provides free kite kits for children to build and decorate and then fly. (Please note: These are only available while supplies last, so it's a good idea to arrive early.)

In addition to flying kites, kids and their families can purchase food from vendors, have their faces painted, or marvel at the creations of a balloon artist. There are often professionals on hand to demonstrate their kite-flying skills, and an opportunity to purchase specialty kites from vendors.

The highlight of the event—assuming the weather permits it—is the Big Kite Candy Drop. A giant kite filled with candy like a piñata flies into the air and drops candy for kids to collect.

Free
CTA bus routes #78, #136, and #146 stop at Marine/Montrose.
Free parking.

BIKE THE DRIVE

Lake Shore Drive between 57th Street/Museum Drive to the south, and Bryn Mawr/Hollywood to the north.
http://www.bikethedrive.org/
Takes place in late May; registration begins in January.

Register and then rise early, because Bike the Drive is a truly unique opportunity. For five hours on a Sunday in May, Lake Shore Drive is closed to cars and will be open to bikes. Roundtrip distance is 30 miles, but registered riders can ride as much or as little as they would like. Three rest stops along the route provide water and snacks. Multiple bike shops make themselves available for free safety checks. Flat tire and minor repairs may be available, but you may be charged for them.

The ride begins at 5:30 a.m., and riders are encouraged to begin no later than 7:00 a.m. Riders can safely enter at Columbus and Jackson, Bryn Mawr rest stop, MSI rest stop, Fullerton checkpoint, and Oakwood checkpoint. Closures along LSD begin at 9:30 a.m., with full closure between 10:30 a.m. and 11:00 a.m. You must be registered to participate, and you must wear a helmet to ride. Bike the Drive takes place rain or shine.

After the ride, Butler Field will have live music, breakfast (for an additional $10 fee), free bike valet, bike-related businesses, and other attractions. The proceeds support the Active Transportation Alliance, which works to make biking, walking, and public transportation easier and safer.

Registration starts at $17 for children 17 or younger and $37–$60 for adults. Children who ride in trailers or bike seats are free, but children on tandem bikes or tagalongs must be registered.

Access to public transportation depends on where you begin the ride. CTA and Metra relax rules for the day and allow bikes on trains and buses.

Discounts are usually offered on parking at Soldier Field's North Garage. Expect to pay about $15.

DO DIVISION STREET FEST

Division Street from Ashland to Leavitt
http://www.do-divisionstreetfest.com/
Takes place in early June for 3 days.

For 362 days a year, Division is just a street; for three days in June, it's a Fest. The Do Division Street Fest takes up ten city blocks of Division, from Ashland to Leavitt, for a sidewalk sale, displays by local vendors, a fashion show (Do Fashion), two live music stages, a family stage, and a Family Fun Fest area. Admission to the Fest is free, and live musical performances on both stages are also free.

A $5 donation is requested for admittance to the Family Fun Fest area. All of the proceeds from this part of the festival go to two local schools. In this area, kids can take pony rides, have their faces painted, make crafts, jump in the bouncy house, and try some basketball or archery in the Sports Zone. There are also performances for families, including story times, live music, magicians, and puppet shows.

Do Division Street Fest is a great way for locals to come together to support the community and for people from other areas to get a taste of Division.

Free admission. $5 recommended donation for the Family Fun Fest.

Take the Blue Line to the Division Street stop.

Street parking available, but may be difficult to find. Parking garages and lots are nearby as well.

PRINTER'S ROW LIT FEST

On Dearborn from Congress to Polk.
http://printersrowlitfest.org/
Takes place in June for 2 days.

The Printer's Row Lit Fest is the largest free outdoor literary event in the Midwest, and each year more than 150,000 people come together to celebrate their love of books. The Fest takes up five blocks of Dearborn, with tents and booths for authors, publishers, booksellers, and other merchants. You'll find discounts on books, book-related merchandise, and authors available to talk to you and sign a copy of their book. More than 200 authors participate in the event in panels, discussions, and in other parts of the Fest. Although admission is free, there are some events that you must purchase tickets to attend. There's also a special part of the Fest for kids; Lil' Lit Park has storytelling, costumed characters, performances, sing-alongs, and other fun stuff for the little ones.

Free

CTA Red Line trains stop at the Harrison Station; Brown, Purple, Orange, and Pink lines stop at the Harold Washington Library. Numerous CTA bus routes stop at State and Balbo, State and Polk, and Clark and Polk.

There are several parking lots in the area; prices will vary.

DRAGON BOAT RACE FOR LITERACY

Ping Tom Memorial Park, 300 W. 19th Street, Chicago, IL 60616
http://chicagochinatown.org/
Late June

The Dragon Boat Race for Literacy kicks off around 8:00 a.m. on a morning in late June, with opening ceremonies starting around 9:00 a.m., and then the race begins. Thirty teams compete annually in the Dragon Boat Race, and proceeds from this event support library programs. Each boat is beautifully decorated to represent a dragon and holds a 20-person team: 1 drummer, 18 paddlers, and 1 flag catcher. The drummer sets the rhythm, and the paddlers paddle in sync. As they approach the finish line, the flag catcher leans forward to grab the flag floating in the water to win the race.

Each year, more than 10,000 people attend this event. There's plenty of food to purchase, and the day is filled with live music, performances of Chinese dances and the Samoan Fire Dance, and martial arts demonstrations. Kids activities include storytelling and arts and crafts.

Free

Parking is very limited. There are some pay lots in the area, but public transportation is probably best.

CTA Red line trains stop at the Cermak-Chinatown station; CTA bus route #62 stops at Archer/Wentworth, and #29 stops at State and 18th Streets.

EYES TO THE SKIES FESTIVAL IN LISLE

Lisle Community Park, 1825 Short Street, Lisle, IL 60532
www.eyestotheskies.org
Takes place in late June/early July. The fest is 3 days long; the carnival is 5 days long.

The 110-acre Lisle Community Park, along with the sky above it, will be full around the Fourth of July with Lisle's annual Eyes to the Skies Festival. Proceeds from the Festival benefit a number of charities. Each year, local businesses offer a huge range of children's activities and live performers entertain the masses. There is a craft fair with 100 booths and a food court.

The highlight of the festival is the 20 or so hot air balloons. Some have businesses advertised on them, some are bright and colorful, and some are even in fun shapes. Each day of the festival there are two launch times—5:30 a.m. and 6:30 p.m. There is no fee to watch the 5:30 a.m. balloon launch. Spectators can also walk on the balloon field to see the balloons up close and talk to the balloon pilots. Tethered balloon rides are offered for $20 per person; rides last about 3–5 minutes and the pilot will take the balloon 20–80 feet high depending on weather conditions. A special balloon called "Serena's Song" is available to do handicapped-accessible tethered rides at no cost. Every evening will start out with balloon launches at 6:30 p.m., followed by balloon glow at 8:15, then a fireworks show.

As you would expect, this festival is very dependent on good weather. Wind and other weather conditions can prevent balloons from launching or cause officials to discontinue tethered rides or prohibit spectators on the balloon field. No refunds are given for admission if weather prevents balloon activities. The Eyes to the Skies Festival covers a large area, so take a look at the map before you arrive. No outside food is allowed in the festival, but you are allowed to bring blankets and lawn chairs.

In addition to the Festival, there is also a carnival that runs for five days. Carnival tickets are $1 each, and each ride requires 3–5 tickets. There is also a Mega Pass that you can purchase to get unlimited rides for the duration of the carnival.

Admission is about $8, cash only; children 6 and younger are free.

The Metra BNSF train line stops at the Lisle station about a mile away.

Free parking in four lots, all with free shuttles. Local businesses often offer paid parking in their lots.

FAMILY FUN FESTIVAL AT MILLENNIUM PARK

Under the tent at the Chase Promenade in Millennium Park, 201 E. Randolph Street, Chicago, IL 60602
https://www.cityofchicago.org/city/en/depts/dca/supp_info/family_fun_festival.html
Takes place daily from late June through late August

It can be hard to keep kids busy all summer and so the city of Chicago and several sponsors have come together to hold the Family Fun Festival at Millennium Park all summer long. The Family Fun Festival is an excellent way to spend time together as a family just having a good time. Every day from 10:00 a.m. to 2:00 p.m. there will be activities and performances for kids of all ages. Storytelling and story times, children's musicians, or dancers take the stage each day to entertain the crowds. Kids can also play with large blocks, get physical with exercises or hula hoops, and play with other kids. Each week features a new Activity Partner, like the Lurie Garden, Lookingglass Theater, or the Museum of Science and Industry. The Activity Partner offers projects for kids to do, so they may plant some seeds, decorate a mask for themselves, or learn a science experiment. There's SO much to do around Millennium Park that starting the summer off here could result in some amazing adventures.

Free

The Metra Electric and South Shore lines stop at Millennium Park Station under Millennium Park. Green, Orange, Brown, Pink, and Purple lines stop at Madison/Wabash and Randolph/Wabash, two blocks away; Red and Blue lines stop at Monroe or Washington, about three blocks away. Multiple CTA buses stop nearby.

Millennium Park, Grant Park North, Grant Park South, and East Monroe parking garages are all available nearby, with rates at about $30–$35.

MILLENNIUM PARK SUMMER FILM SERIES

Jay Pritzker Pavilion at Millennium Park, 201 E. Randolph St., Chicago, IL 60602
https://www.cityofchicago.org/city/en/depts/dca/supp_info/millennium_park7
.html
Takes place from late June to late August, with one film offered each week.

Nighttime in Chicago is magical with the twinkling lights of the skyline and the lapping of the waves on the lakeshore. Make it even more fun by spending a few hours under the stars watching a movie. Grab a seat in the Jay Pritzker Pavilion, or you can spread out a blanket or chairs on the Great Lawn. Bring your own snacks and drinks or purchase them nearby. Movies are shown on a 40-foot LED screen on Tuesday nights beginning at 6:30 p.m. There are a variety of movies shown during the film series, so some may not be appropriate for young children. In the past, movies in the film series have included *Ferris Bueller's Day Off, West Side Story, Thelma and Louise, Moonstruck,* and *Finding Nemo.*

If you're looking for more outdoor movies, the Chicago Park District also hosts Movies in the Parks each summer. More than 250 outdoor screenings are scheduled in parks around the city, with a variety of movies both current and classic. See a full list of movies offered on the Chicago Park District website.

Free

The Metra Electric and South Shore lines stop at Millennium Park Station under Millennium Park. Green, Orange, Brown, Pink, and Purple lines stop at Madison/Wabash and Randolph/Wabash, two blocks away; Red and Blue lines stop at Monroe or Washington, about three blocks away. Multiple CTA buses stop nearby.

Millennium Park, Grant Park North, Grant Park South, and East Monroe parking garages are all available nearby, with rates at about $30–$35.

CHICAGO BEARS TRAINING CAMP

Olivet Nazarene University, 1 University Drive, Bourbonnais, IL
(224) 795-1178
http://www.chicagobears.com/events/training-camp.html
Late July through early August

Chicago Bears tickets can be hard to get, and they're expensive. If you want to see the players in action for free, you'll want to visit the Chicago Bears Training Camp in Bourbonnais. Yes, it's a sixty-mile drive from Chicago, but the experience will be well worth the road trip. Pack up the kids, some snacks, and a cooler of water and you're all set. Check the Chicago Bears Training Camp schedule on their website for exact days and times. Practices start at 9:35 a.m. or 11:30 a.m. and last for about 2 hours. There's food available for purchase, or you can bring your own cooler, and be sure to bring sun protection because there's not much shade.

There is a special area set up for kids with fun activities like bouncy houses, and there are also themed practice days.

BUD BILLIKEN PARADE
The parade starts at King Drive and Oakton Blvd and ends at Garfield Blvd (55th Street) and Elsworth Drive. The celebration after the parade takes place at Washington Park.
http://www.budbillikenparade.org/
The parade takes place on the second Saturday in August.

The Bud Billiken Parade has been a Chicago tradition for more than 85 years and is the largest African-American parade in the country. Created and produced by the Chicago Defender Charities, the Bud Billiken Parade started to provide underprivileged children with a chance to be in the limelight. Because it takes place in August every year, this is a great end-of-summer/back-to-school event, with floats, marching bands, performers, and celebrities.

The parade marches from Bronzeville to Washington Park. Specifically, it goes south on King Drive from Oakwood to 51st Street and continues on Elsworth through Washington Park to Garfield/55th Street. The parade is broadcast live on ABC 7.

The parade is followed by a picnic at Washington Park, with treats and give-aways, activities, special guests, and sometimes a concert.

CHICAGO AIR & WATER SHOW
North Avenue Beach, 1600 N. Lake Shore Drive, Chicago, IL 60613
http://www.cityofchicago.org/city/en/depts/dca/supp_info/chicago_air_and_watershow.html
Weekend in mid to late August

The Chicago Air & Water Show, the largest show of its type in the country, takes place for one weekend in August. Performances are about 5 hours long and take place on Saturday and again on Sunday. Spectators watch daredevil pilots, parachute teams, jets flying in formation, water-skiing, and boat jumping. Both military and civilian pilots participate, and most of the planes in the show operate out of the Gary, Indiana, airport for the weekend. Performers include: U.S. Navy Blue Angels, Parachute Teams from the Army and Navy, The Firebirds Delta Team, Team AeroDynamix, the Chicago Fire Department Air/Sea Rescue, and lots, lots more. Be aware that although the performers are experts, accidents can (and do) happen. Grandstands are set up at North Avenue Beach, and it's the best place to see the show, but if you can't make it there (it gets pretty crowded), you can still get a good view along the lakeshore from Oak Street Beach to Fullerton, or at Ohio Street Beach. Spectators are welcome to bring chairs, blankets, and coolers, and there is also food for sale at the show. Pack a bag! You'll want to have sunscreen, water, snacks, ear protection, and binoculars.

Free

CTA bus route #151 stops at Lake Shore and North Avenue near North Avenue Beach.

Millennium Park Garage offers a free shuttle to North Avenue Beach; expect to pay $35–$40 for parking.

DAY OUT WITH THOMAS

Illinois Railway Museum, 7000 Olson Road, Union, IL 60180
http://www.thomastrainride.com/
Takes place in August for a couple weekends

This is a big event every year, with tickets selling like hotcakes. Every little one who has ever wanted to see Thomas the Train in real life now has a chance to do that. The Thomas engine (and Percy engine) arrive at the Illinois Railway Museum once a summer for two weekends of Thomas-themed festivities. Kids can meet Sir Topham Hatt, watch Thomas the Train videos and hear Thomas the Train stories, play with Thomas the Train toys, and get a Thomas the Train temporary tattoo. There are plenty of vendors selling Thomas the Train merchandise and other toys and goodies the kids will want you to buy. Clowns, magicians, and other live performers will be there to provide entertainment.

At your scheduled time, you'll board a train pulled by the Thomas the Train engine. Everyone wants to be in the front to be closer to the Thomas engine, but head toward the middle or back. Once you're on the train, you won't be able to see Thomas anyway, but if you're farther back you'll be able to get some glimpses of Thomas as you round corners.

Ticket prices include one scheduled ride on a Thomas train and admission to the Illinois Railway Museum for the day.

About $20 per person for admission and a ride on the Thomas train. Additional tickets are available for about $10 per person to ride on the Percy train. Children under age 2 do not need a ticket.

There is no public transportation available nearby.

Free parking in lot.

COMIC CON

Donald E. Stephens Convention Center, 5555 North River Road, Rosemont, IL 60018

http://wizardworld.com/comiccon/chicago

Takes place in late August for one long weekend (Thursday through Sunday)

Comic Con has a food court, vendors selling comic-related merchandise, artists selling their own work, and booths for actors and celebrities. You can purchase rare comics or a funny t-shirt, meet your favorite cartoonist or discover a new artist, and meet people who play your favorite characters on TV and in the movies. There are panels and discussions, but some of these require an additional ticket to attend. There are also some actors you can approach and request an autograph from for free and others for whom you must pay a fee in order to obtain an autograph or photo. Prices vary, but there are some VIP passes available on the Wizard World Comic Con website.

Comic Con is better than Halloween; many people dress in very elaborate and impressive costumes of their favorite comic book characters. Most of these people love posing for pictures with kids because they love it that kids see them as that character.

General admission tickets are about $40; each paying adult can bring in two children ages 10 or under for free.

Multiple Pace bus routes stop at River/Williams and at River/Bryn Mawr.

Parking is located in the garage across from the center, directly behind the Embassy Suites Hotel O'Hare and costs $15.

MIDNIGHT CIRCUS IN THE PARKS

Chicago Park District Parks

http://midnightcircus.net

Takes place August through October

Any park is a favorite destination for most kids, but what would make them even better? Each summer a circus tent pops up in local parks in Chicago. Acrobats, aerialists, contortionists, and other amazing performers (including some kids! And a dog!) surprise and delight crowds of all ages, and all the proceeds go to help the parks. Shows last about 90 minutes, and there are refreshments available for purchase.

Midnight Circus in the Parks originally started in 2007 in an effort to save a local playground. After the tremendous success of the first year, they continued to expand to additional parks and have raised over $850,000 so far for local park improvements.

Tickets are $5–$20; children under age 2 are free.
Public transportation and parking vary by location.

FESTIVAL DE LA VILLITA (LITTLE VILLAGE FESTIVAL)

Little Village, 26th Street and Kostner Avenue, Chicago, IL 60623
https://www.everfest.com/e/chicago-cinco-de-mayo-festival-and-parade-chicago-il
Takes place in September and lasts three days

It's not surprising that Chicago's Little Village neighborhood—a Mexican-American community sometimes referred to as the "Mexico of the Midwest"—hosts one of the largest Mexican American celebrations in the Heartland. For more than 25 years the Festival de La Villita has been celebrating Mexican heritage and the independence of Mexico from Spain achieved in September 1810. Count on musical entertainment, carnival rides, and lots of food from local vendors serving South-of-the-Border specialties. In the past, the festival has also included a concert, for which tickets must be purchased. The festival culminates in a Sunday afternoon parade—the 26th Street Mexican Independence Day Parade. A portion of the proceeds of the event go to support community programs and services of the Little Village Chamber of Commerce.

Free
CTA bus route #60 stops at 26th Street/Kostner.
Limited street parking is available.

ST. CHARLES SCARECROW FESTIVAL
101-119 N. 3rd Street, St. Charles, IL 60174
http://scarecrowfest.com/
Takes place in early October and lasts about three days

For more than 25 years St. Charles has been hosting a special autumn event—the Scarecrow Festival. Live musical performances, a carnival, petting zoo, and an arts and crafts show are on the schedule each year, as well as a number of activities for kids, including gymnastics performances, magic shows, sidewalk chalk art, and a balloon artist. You'll definitely need to get some snacks or food between all those activities, and there are plenty of vendors selling festival foods.

Of course, it wouldn't be a Scarecrow Festival without a few scarecrows—or maybe more than 100 of them! You can vote for your favorite scarecrow, and cash prizes are awarded to winners in five different categories. You can bring some old clothes to the fest to make your own scarecrow to take home, but why not sign up before the Fest to enter one in the contest? Get creative, because prizes can be as much as $550!

Free
There is no public transportation available nearby.
Free parking.

CHICAGO ARCHITECTURE FOUNDATION'S ANNUAL OPEN HOUSE
200 different sites in Chicago
http://openhousechicago.org/
One weekend in mid-October

Chicago is a wonderland for architecture and design enthusiasts on a normal day, but for a weekend in October it gets even better. Open House Chicago, offered by the Chicago Architecture Foundation, provides a behind-the-scenes look at 150 Chicago structures. You can go inside the McCormick Bridgehouse to see the massive gears, go onstage at the Jay Pritzker Pavilion, check out the beautifully restored Firehouse Chicago, and lots more! The Open House Chicago site has a list of all the participating buildings, and you can easily search by neighborhood or by categories. One of the category options is "family-friendly," making it easy to find places to visit with kids. In fact, one of the family-friendly options in 2016 was the Big Monster Door at Big Monster Toys. What's behind that door? Visitors are only admitted one weekend out of the year to find out!

Free
Public transportation and parking vary by location.

CHICAGO TOY & GAME FAIR
Navy Pier, 600 E. Grand Avenue, Chicago, IL 60611
http://www.chitagfair.com/
One weekend in mid to late November

The Chicago Toy & Game Fair is an annual event that brings toy and game makers, both new and old, to Navy Pier. You'll find major brands (like sponsors Mayfair Games, Hasbro, and Razor) and independent toy inventors. Roam the giant convention hall to see and test out all kinds of toys, meet toy inventors (including the inventors of Rainbow Loom and Jenga), participate in gaming tournaments, and see yo-yo champions perform. ChiTAG is scheduled just before Black Friday, so you can discover and test out new toys before you buy; some vendors even offer special pricing if you buy at the event. For extra fun, reserve your spot at the Star Wars Luncheon.

$5/child, $10/adult. Children under 3 are free.

CTA bus routes #29 State Street, #65 Grand Avenue, #66 Chicago Avenue, and #124 Navy Pier Express (serving Metra lines, Millennium Park/Randolph Street, Ogilvie and Union stations) will take you to Navy Pier. The #2 Hyde Park Express also serves Navy Pier.

Parking in the Navy Pier parking garages is $25. If they are full, you can also park at Grand Plaza Park (540 N. State) or Ogden Plaza Self Park (300 E. North Water Street) for $15 with validation from Navy Pier; both are less than half a mile away and you can walk or take a trolley (seasonally) to Navy Pier.

CHRISTMAS AROUND THE WORLD AND HOLIDAY OF LIGHTS AT THE MUSEUM OF SCIENCE AND INDUSTRY

5700 S. Lake Shore Drive, Chicago, IL 60637
(773) 684-1414
www.msichicago.org
Takes place mid-November to January

The Museum of Science and Industry brings an entire forest indoors to celebrate Christmas. Volunteers from communities throughout Chicago decorate trees to represent their country or culture, and these 50 trees are displayed at the MSI during the holiday season, surrounding the museum's four-story Grand Tree in the Rotunda. While families marvel at the beautiful lights and decorations, they can also learn about the Ukrainian fable about a Christmas tree decorated with spider webs, see origami created by local Girl Scouts for the tree representing China, and discover how Hungary decorates its trees with cookies, candies, and fruit. And every thirty minutes it "snows" indoors in the Rotunda! Each year has a theme that coincides with a current exhibit at the museum. Past themes have included the comic *Peanuts,* Disney, and Robotics.

The Holiday of Lights celebrates holidays focused on light or enlightenment. Traditions of Chinese New Year, Diwali, Hanukkah, Kwanzaa, Visakha Puja Day, Ramadan, and St. Lucia Day are featured in a digital presentation.

Everything is included in **general admission,** which is $18 for adults, $11 for children ages 3–11 years old.

Metra Electric Line and South Shore Line trains stop at the 55th/56th/57th Street station two blocks away. CTA bus route #2 Hyde Park Express stops at 57th and Stony Island; route #6 Jackson Park Express stops at 56th Street and Hyde Park.

Parking in the underground garage at the museum is $22.

WINTER WONDERFEST AT NAVY PIER

Navy Pier, 600 E. Grand Avenue, Chicago, IL 60611
https://navypier.com/winter-wonderfest/
Takes place in December and early January.

There are amazing holiday activities in Chicago, but most of them are outdoors. If you just can't brave the cold, head to Navy Pier, where they have a plethora of winter activities and they're all indoors. There are 28 different activities, from fun photo ops, to a 50-foot-tall Ferris wheel, to a 15-foot-tall "snow" tubing hill and ice rink. The kids can meet Santa, bounce in inflatables, and ride on carnival rides in this winter wonderland. There will be a fireworks show to celebrate the New Year.

There are height restrictions for each of the rides, but there is something for kids of all ages. See the Winter Wonderfest website for a detailed list. Family ticket bundles are available at a discounted price. A coat check is available for $5 a coat; there is no bag check.

Tickets are $10 for a mini-pass or $25 for an activity pass that includes access to all rides and activities. Children under 36" do not need a paid ticket

CTA bus routes #29 State Street, #65 Grand Avenue, #66 Chicago Avenue, and #124 Navy Pier Express (serving Metra lines, Millennium Park/Randolph Street, Ogilvie and Union stations) will take you to Navy Pier. The #2 Hyde Park Express also serves Navy Pier.

Parking in the Navy Pier parking garages is $25.

CHICAGO TROLLEY HOLIDAY LIGHTS TOUR

Tours start at the John Hancock Center, 875 N. Michigan Avenue, Chicago, IL 60611
(773) 648-5000
http://chicagotrolley.com/?r=3
Takes place from Thanksgiving until Christmas

Chicago has some amazing lights and displays during the holiday season, but it can be difficult to see them all by car, on foot, or with public transportation. The solution is the Chicago Trolley Holiday Lights Tour, where someone else does the driving and you can focus on observing the magical sights of the holidays. Your journey begins at the John Hancock Center and continues for two and a half hours throughout the city, from the Gold Coast, to State Street and through the Loop, to Christkindlmarket at Daley Plaza, up to Lincoln Park's ZooLights, and finally back to the John Hancock Center. Along the way there are two places where you can hop off to do more exploring, and you'll be treated to a special holiday cupcake from the legendary Sprinkles bakery.

There are a limited number of tickets available, so purchasing tickets in advance is a good idea. Got a large crowd? Private rentals are available.

Tickets are $29 for adults, $18 for children 5–15 years old.

CTA #125 Water Tower Express bus stops at the John Hancock Building.

Parking at the John Hancock Center garage is about $35.

ILLUMINATION AT THE MORTON ARBORETUM

4100 IL-53, Lisle, IL 60532
(630) 968-0074
http://www.mortonarb.org/events/illumination-tree-lights-morton-arboretum
Takes place from mid-November to early January

The Morton Arboretum is always a beautiful place to visit, but they kick it up a few notches during Illumination, giving you an opportunity to see trees in a different light (or lights). Fifty acres of trees are adorned with twinkling lights along a one-mile path. Illumination is more than just some holiday lights—it's an art installation and interactive experience, with projections and unexpected displays (like lights on the surface of the lake). Along the path, visitors stop to push buttons, turn wheels, hug trees, or sing to a tree, and the trees respond with changing lights.

Bundle up for the weather; there are warming stations and fires along the way, but you'll probably be outside 90 minutes, and don't worry if there's snow—it'll make the displays even more beautiful. They sell hot chocolate along the path, so bring some cash, and a stroller is a good idea if you've got a little one who might get tired along the way.

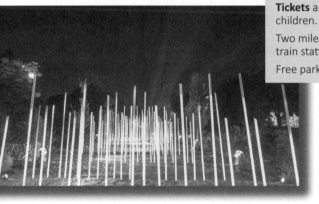

Tickets are $18–$22 for adults; $12–$14 for children.

Two miles from the Burlington Northern Metra train station.

Free parking.

CHRISTKINDLMARKET

Daley Plaza, 50 W. Washington, Chicago, IL 60602
http://www.christkindlmarket.com/
Takes place for part of November and most of December. Open daily from about 11:00 a.m. until 8:00 or 9:00 p.m.

Celebrate the holiday season with a visit to Christkindlmarket, a traditional German holiday market with vendors from around the world. Christkindlmarket is an open-air market, with shops for gifts and specialty items and traditional German food and drinks. There's live music and entertainment, and Santa even keeps a house here! Not only do you get to experience German traditions, but many of the vendors speak German, so students of the language can have a chance to practice their skills.

Kinder Korner offers activities and events for children at Christkindlmarket. You can print out a scavenger hunt list (in English or German!) to complete at the market, and while you're there, kids can pick up a Passport and Activity Book. After getting five stamps at booths with "Passport Stamping Station" signs, kids can be entered to win prizes. Kids 14 and under can sign up for the Kinder Klub and receive special benefits via email.

Check the Christkindlmarket website for a schedule of special events, including a visit from Christkind, a fairy-like character from German folklore who is similar to Santa Claus.

The location is ideal if you'd like to follow up your visit with some sightseeing and touring the holiday windows and lights. There is also a Christkindlmarket in Naperville. Because these are outdoor markets, extremely cold weather or storms can sometimes cause them to close.

Free

The CTA Blue Line train stops at Washington/Dearborn, and the Red Line stops at State/Lake. Several CTA bus routes serve this area.

There are several parking garages in this area. The City of Chicago recommends using SpotHero to reserve a parking space.

POLAR EXPRESS

Fox River Valley Trolley Museum, 365 S La Fox St, South Elgin, IL 60177
Union Station, 225 S. Canal Street, Chicago, IL 60606
http://www.raileventsinc.com/polar-express
Dates for this event vary according to location, but usually occur during the month of December.

Based on *The Polar Express* movie, the Polar Express Train Ride takes children (and their parents) on a magical holiday journey. Riders will experience the sounds of the movie during their ride, and there will be a reading of *The Polar Express* book. Hot chocolate and cookies are served on the train, and when the train arrives at the "North Pole," Santa will board the train and present each child with their own sleigh bell. Rides last about 60–75 minutes, round trip, and pajamas are encouraged for this event!

Keep in mind that it will likely be cold while you wait for the train, so bundle up, especially if you're wearing pjs. Locations can vary each year, but both the Fox River Trolley Museum in South Elgin and Union Station in Chicago have hosted this event for the past couple years.

Tickets are about $55 for adults and $40 for children ages 2–11 years old. Children under 2 do not need a ticket if they sit on a parent's lap. Tickets for this event often go on sale in August and sell out very quickly.

Free parking at Fox River Trolley Museum. There are parking garages in the area of Union Station, but it's much more convenient to take public transportation.

Misc Free Activities

- **Visit Chicago filming sites**—Many great movies were filmed in Chicago and the suburbs. Take a day to visit some of the filming sites for movies like *The Breakfast Club; Home Alone; The Blues Brothers; Ferris Bueller's Day Off; Backdraft; The Dark Knight; Groundhog Day; Planes, Trains, and Automobiles; Sixteen Candles;* and *Uncle Buck.*

- **Chicago Greeter**—Take a free custom tour with a Chicago Greeter volunteer to one of 25 different Chicago neighborhoods, or see lots of sites in the city in your area of interest (such as family-friendly, art and architecture, or foodie spots).

- **Free Museum Days**—Chicago is full of great museums and zoos, and if you're an Illinois resident, you can take advantage of Free Museum Days. Dates vary by museum/attraction.

- **Chicago Public Libraries**—Chicago Public Libraries offer countless services, programs, and events. Check out your local city (or suburban) library for events or take a trip to the mother of all Chicago area libraries—Harold Washington Library.

- **Kidical Mass**—Kidical Mass organizes family-friendly bike rides through Chicago neighborhoods.

- **Appreciate Chicago Art**—There's no need to step into a museum—there's art all around in Chicago. The Chicago Public Art Guide provides information about each piece; take a trek around the city to find your favorites.

DAY TRIPS AND GETAWAYS

Sometimes you need to get away, but a long-distance trip just isn't practical. Luckily, there are plenty of places within just a couple hours' drive that are ideal if you're looking to relax and rejuvenate, or adventure and energize. Perfect for a weekend visit, or just a day trip, these can be destinations for Chicago locals or a nice stopover in or out of town for travelers.

✳ LAKE GENEVA, WI ✳

Lake Geneva, in southern Wisconsin, has a long history as a resort town, with prominent families like the Wrigleys (Wrigley's Gum) and the Mortons (Morton Salt) owning property there. You don't need a fortune to enjoy all that Lake Geneva has to offer.

WHERE TO STAY

Lake Geneva has lodging options for most budgets and resorts with unique amenities from full spas to family water parks.

If location is key, **The Cove** is the place to be. It's located just across from the lakeshore, with a park and gazebo in between, and it's just a short walk away from restaurants, shopping, Riviera Beach, and boat rentals. The Cove is condo suites with one or two bedrooms and a kitchen. There's a restaurant on-site, and three pools—one indoors and two outdoors.

Timber Ridge is a short drive from the lakeshore, but it offers just about everything a family could want. The suites here have private bedrooms and full kitchens, complete with essentials like dishes, utensils, and pots and pans. There's a large 50,000-square-foot indoor/outdoor waterpark with slides, a lazy river, an activity pool, and even a "Tiny Timbers" area for young children. With an arcade, spa, restaurants, and nearby horse stables, everyone in the family will have plenty to do.

The Abbey is another option for families. Although it's not in Lake Geneva, it's just a 20-minute drive away, in Fontana, WI, and The Abbey is the only full-service resort on Lake Geneva. There are indoor and outdoor pools, a spa, a private dock, multiple dining options, and a complimentary shuttle to downtown Lake Geneva. The Abbey also schedules family-friendly activities like bonfires, movie nights, and crafts for kids.

WHAT TO DO

The obvious activity in Lake Geneva is the beach. **Riviera Beach** has bathrooms and lifeguards, and it's very well-maintained. You do have to pay for access, but you can bring in coolers, chairs, and all your other beach necessities (except for glass bottles).

If you really love the water, consider renting a boat or other watercraft. **Gage Marine** rents standup paddleboats and kayaks, and **Marina Bay Boat Rentals** has speed boats, pontoon boats, and wave runners. In the winter, you can rent skis and snowboards from **Mountain Top at Lake Geneva.**

For a day of free sightseeing, stroll part of the 26-mile **Geneva Lake Shore Path** that runs through the backyards of beautiful mansions on the lakeshore. Originally used by the Potawatomi tribe, the path remains because of regulations that 20 feet leading to the lakeshore is public domain. You can start from any of four entry points and walk as much or as little of the trail as you want and enjoy the amazing views of Lake Geneva on one side and impressive homes on the other. The path is family-friendly, but not suitable for strollers.

Learn more about the lake and properties on a boat tour such as the Ice Cream Social offered by **Lake Geneva Cruise Line.** They also have a U.S. Mailboat Tour where passengers watch as an agile mailperson delivers mail to 60 homes around the lake by jumping on and off the boat while it's moving. During the holidays, take a Santa Cruise.

Or, if you're looking for something really different, head to nearby **Delavan,** where you can see a Vegas-style dancing horses show at the **Dancing Horses Theatre & Animal Gardens Petting Zoo.** The 90-minute show is unique, and dining options are available. There are also farm and exotic animals to see here, and you can take a train ride through **Wildlife Park.**

WHERE TO EAT

They say breakfast is the most important meal of the day so you might as well start with something yummy. **Simple Café** offers a large menu of standard and original breakfast dishes, including a chicken chorizo chili omelet and a seasonal harvest frittata, and they use local ingredients and maintain close relationships with their farmer suppliers. The kids' menu has standard favorites (pancakes and omelets), and a couple choices for little foodies (a chicken bowl dish and an artisan mac and cheese).

If you're spending the day downtown or on the beach, **Popeye's** is convenient for lunch or dinner. Popeye's has a huge dining room that can seat over 500 people and an outdoor patio for warm months. They're just across from the lake and offer a relaxed and fun atmosphere. Their specialty is their outdoor rotisserie, but they also serve seafood, pasta, burgers, and sandwiches, and they have a children's menu. Popeye's sometimes has balloon artists working in the restaurant in the evenings.

Pizza is something everyone can agree on, so **Oakfire Restaurant & Pizzeria,** which serves Napoletana style pizza, is a great choice for a family meal. Kids get coloring menus, crayons, and pizza dough to keep them busy. Oakfire has a kids' menu and the Mickey Mouse pizza is a big hit among their younger customers.

✴ SOUTH HAVEN, MI ✴

South Haven, a.k.a. "South Heaven" to many of its visitors, is a south-western Michigan beach town about two hours from Chicago. There are seven beaches, but the two largest (and most popular) ones are North Beach and South Beach. Both are equipped with bathroom facilities, parking, and concessions. Visitors love to spend the day at the beach, boating on the lake, or walking along the pier that holds the world-fa-mous South Haven Lighthouse that dates back to the 1870s and is still ac-tive in aiding navigation. The lighthouse is about 35 feet tall and although you can't go inside, you can walk to the end of the pier for beautiful views.

WHERE TO STAY

South Haven has lots of lodging choices, including chain hotels, resorts, cab-ins, and bed & breakfasts. Stick to a tight budget by staying at a chain hotel, such as the **Hampton Inn, Holiday Inn Express & Suites,** or **Baymont Inn & Suites.** Each offers free parking, wifi, and breakfast, as well as an indoor pool. Prices start at about $100, $90, and $75, respectively, and each has options for families (either suites or adjoining rooms) available.

If you prefer something with a little more character, **Lake Bluff Inn & Suites** has an outdoor pool, complimentary continental breakfast, views of **Lake Michi-gan** (although no lake access), and they have both rooms and suites available. Rates start at about $75.

There's also the **Sun & Sand Resort,** a 1920s farm resort with three differ-ent lodging buildings. On the spacious grounds, you'll find an outdoor saltwater pool, fire pit, nature trail, pond beach, and a waterfall. Connecting rooms are available, and some rooms have kitchenettes. Rates start at about $120.

Renting a home is another option, especially if you're traveling with a large family or a group. Locations, sizes, prices, and amenities vary a great deal. **Bluewater Vacation Rentals, Lakeshore Lodging, Michigan Vacation Rentals,** and **Shores Vacation Rentals** are just a few places to start looking for the perfect place to stay.

WHAT TO DO

Families can enjoy the simple things—like kayaking on the lake or visiting farms and farm stands selling fresh fruits and vegetables. South Haven has several U-pick farms with a variety of produce. **DeGrandchamp Farms** is famous for its blueberries; **Overhisen Orchards** has cherries, peaches, apricots, pears, plums, apples, and pumpkins; and **Stephenson Farms** has blueberries, sweet corn, apples, pumpkins, squash, and gourds.

South Haven has miles of trails for hiking, biking, and horseback riding. The **Van Buren State Park** has dune formations and a mile of sandy beach on its 400 acres, and there are campsites. The **Kal-Haven Trail** is a popular spot for outdoor enthusiasts with 34 miles perfect for biking, hiking, cross-country skiing, or snowmobiling. You'll journey past farm lands, wooded areas, rivers and streams, and even through a covered bridge.

If you want a little more adventure, you can take in a race at the **GingerMan Raceway,** where you can be a spectator (or a driver if you have the experience or a coach) during their races and open race days. Or, **KJC ATV Rental** provides everything you need for a muddy expedition in the woods—ATVs, helmets, trails designed for ATVs, and even some instruction and tips.

May to October is peak travel season in South Haven, but that doesn't mean that you can't have plenty of fun in the colder months. The **South Haven Ice Rink** is open from late November to mid-March, and day passes are only $4. Skate rental is available and although the rink is outdoors, it is covered by a pavilion roof and has a cooling system for the ice, so they are open snow or shine. Need a little more speed? KJC ATV Rental also rents snowmobiles. They don't have scheduled hours during the winter, but you can call to make arrangements. There's also the **Michigan Theatre,** offering first-run movies and concessions at old-fashioned prices; two people can see a movie here and get concessions for the cost of a single movie ticket at many Chicago theaters.

WHERE TO EAT

South Haven has a number of restaurants serving different types of food. Some of the family-friendly restaurants include Never Miss Café, Clementine's, and Subs N More. **Never Miss Café** is a friendly little restaurant that is a favorite among locals; stop here for breakfast or lunch. **Clementine's** is located in the downtown area in a beautiful old bank building filled with antiques and black-and-white pictures. Lunch and dinner are served at Clementine's, and they have a large kids' menu. **Subs N More** doesn't look like much, but the food is yummy, and the kids will love stopping here for pizza or sub sandwiches (and adults won't mind either—they have a huge selection of sandwiches). Eat in or grab some subs to go for the beach.

✳ MILWAUKEE, WI ✳

Milwaukee is the largest city in Wisconsin and is known for its breweries and festivals. Milwaukee has lodging and dining of every kind, as well as countless art, science, and history museums and performing arts venues of all types and sizes. The two-mile RiverWalk in the heart of the city is fun for families because it's lined with public art to explore and takes you past some of the best restaurants and shops in Milwaukee.

WHERE TO STAY

The Brewhouse Inn & Suites is a boutique hotel in what used to be an abandoned Pabst Brewery. In repurposing the building, the owners maintained many of the features of the brewery, including brickwork, arched doorways, a spiral staircase, and copper kettles. There are studio, one-bedroom, and two-bedroom suites to choose from, and each one has a unique layout and a full kitchen! There's no pool, but complimentary breakfast is available and older kids will love the cool factor. Rates start at about $190.

If you're looking for something a little more economical, consider the **Hilton Garden Inn Milwaukee Downtown.** The location is convenient, and they offer rooms and suites, both with a microwave and refrigerator. Breakfast is offered daily and in-room dining is available in the evening. There's a fitness center, but no pool. Rates start at about $100.

Residence Inn Milwaukee Downtown has one and two bedroom suites with fully equipped kitchens in addition to standard rooms. Complimentary hot breakfast and the location near the **Riverwalk** and other attractions will get your day started out right. Rates start at about $100.

WHAT TO DO

For hands-on and interactive playing and learning with kids, visit the **Betty Brinn Children's Museum.** Designed for kids 10 and under, the museum gives kids an opportunity to work at a global communications company in the Word Headquarters exhibit, learn about health and nutrition in the Kohl's Healthy Kids: It's Your Move! exhibit, and explore all the businesses in the kid-size Home Town. Toddlers and preschoolers will love Pocket Park, a playground just for them with a treehouse and slide, produce stand and garden, and a soft play area.

If you want to try something a little different, why not do a family outing to a brewery? **Sprecher's Brewery** offers tours for about $8 for adults and $5 for kids. The tours are pretty short—about 15 or 20 minutes—and afterwards you move on to sampling. Adults get four beer samples; but everyone gets as many soda samples as they'd like.

How does **Milwaukee County Zoo** compare to Brookfield Zoo or Lincoln Park Zoo? Find out! They have over 2,000 animals, and you can explore the grounds on foot, by Safari Train, by Ski Safari, or by Zoomobile. You can also feed the giraffes or catch a show at the Kohl's Wild Theater.

Learn all about history at the **Milwaukee Public Museum.** Three floors of exhibits include dioramas of Africa and the Arctic, the streets of old Milwaukee, and the skeleton of a Hebior Mammoth. The Milwaukee Public Museum also has the Puelicher Butterfly Wing, where you can walk among butterflies in a greenhouse garden, and the Dome Theater, where you can see 2-D and 3-D movies on a dome six stories high.

WHERE TO EAT

Mader's serves traditional German food in a large and impressive dining room filled with German art and antiques. They boast many celebrity diners, including three U.S. presidents, Cary Grant, John Belushi, Katie Perry, Justin Beiber, and Usher. They have a kids' menu and a large selection of dishes for brunch, lunch, and dinner. It's not an inexpensive place; if you don't want to spring for a pricey meal, just visit for a snack—they have a giant pretzel served with dipping sauces that can feed a couple of people. (It's not on the menu, but just ask!)

Spoiler warning: This next recommendation is NOT for people with peanut allergies or sensitivities. **A.J. Bombers** is a burger joint with some seriously good burgers. In fact, they won a burger battle on the Travel Channel's *Food Wars*. The food is good and kids will love that they can write on the walls and throw peanut shells on the floor. Also cool: the peanuts are delivered to your table via peanut bombs from the ceiling.

Your mission—should you choose to accept it—is to have a meal at the **Safe-House.** You'll need a password to get in (or a willingness to complete a challenge) plus $5 per person and a sense of adventure. Your experience at Safe-House will be memorable, but it must remain top secret. Current intel indicates there will be a SafeHouse in Chicago soon.

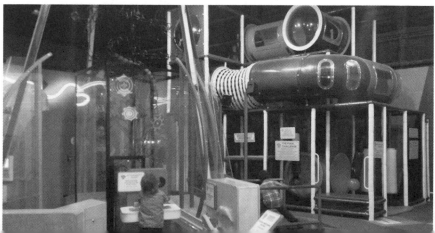

STARVED ROCK STATE PARK ✳ UTICA, IL

Starved Rock State Park is known for the amazing rock formations and 18 canyons found on its 2,500+ acres. Over 2 million visitors come each year to admire the natural beauty and hike the trails of the park. You can also work in visits to Matthiessen State Park and Buffalo Rock State Park, which are both within a couple of miles.

WHERE TO STAY

The **Starved Rock Lodge** is located in **Starved Rock State Park** and has the rustic decor of a log cabin but all the modern conveniences you could want. There's an indoor pool and a children's pool, a restaurant and café on-site, and free wifi. Indoor and outdoor activities are on the activity calendar, so if you want to see a live concert, enjoy a massage, or take a guided hike, they have you covered. Cabins are available for rent as well, and the state park is just outside your door.

Just a couple miles from the Starved Rock Lodge is **Grizzly Jack's Grand Bear Resort,** which boasts huge indoor water and amusement parks. Grizzly Jack's offers hotel suites, vacation villas, and luxury cabins, so whether you're booking a stay for two or for 18, there are accommodations that will be just right. With a restaurant, sweet shop, and café, and complete kitchens in villas and cabins, you won't have to leave the grounds for a meal if you don't want to. Not that the kids would ever get bored with the waterpark or indoor amusement park, but if they did there's still mini golf, a playground, and an arcade.

Holiday Inn Express Hotel and Suites in Peru is conveniently located just off of I-80 and is about a 20-minute drive from Starved Rock, Matthiessen State Park, and Buffalo Rock State Park. A complimentary hot breakfast is served each morning, and there is an indoor pool. Rates start at about $90.

WHAT TO DO

At **Matthiessen State Park** you'll find five miles of hiking trails with options for both easy hiking routes and more difficult trails for advanced hikers. There are steep cliffs and deep canyons, so it can be dangerous.

Matthiessen also has a field archery range, six miles of cross-country ski trails (ski rentals available), and nine miles of mountain bike and horseback riding trails.

Starved Rock State Park is filled with canyons and majestic bluffs. There are 13 miles of hiking trails open year-round. Trail maps and signs help guide hikers along the way. The Starved Rock Lodge also offers trolley tours throughout the year—**Eagle Tours** in the winter, **Waterfalls & Canyon Tours** in the spring, **Fall Colors Tours** in autumn, and a **Christmas Lights Tour** in the winter.

It's always a good idea to check the Starved Rock or Matthiessen website or call for hiking conditions and potential closures because of weather conditions before you visit.

For a fun indoor activity, visit **Enchanted Forest Indoor Amusement Park** at Grizzly Jack's Grand Bear Resort. Guests of the resort receive passes as part of their stay; visitors who are not staying can purchase a pass. Enchanted Forest has children's rides, bounce houses, a rope course, and adult rides like a Tilt-A-Whirl, Vertical Plunge, the Growler, and Grizzly.

WHERE TO EAT

Utica isn't a big city, but that doesn't mean they don't have tasty dining options. **Skoog's Pub and Grill** is a relaxed restaurant where you can get traditional American pub food like burgers and wings, as well as tacos, ribs, and fish. There's a kids' menu and daily specials.

Nonie's Bakery Café is another comfortable place to grab some good food. They serve breakfast and lunch and sell a variety of cakes, pastries, and home-made bread. Nonie's is sunny and homey and feels like you're having a bite in a friend's home. They have a kids' menu and books and games are available for kids to use.

If you want to try something a little different, **Ron's Cajun Connection** serves "swamp to table" Cajun food made from fresh ingredients. Gumbo, po' boys, chicken, steak, catfish, frog legs—it's all available here, and Cajun Ron stops by the tables to make sure everyone's enjoying the food. Alligator po' boy anyone?

✷ INDEX ✷